Charter Schools

Other Books of Related Interest:

Opposing Viewpoints Series

For-Profit Education

Juvenile Crime

School Funding

Street Teens

Teenage Sexuality

At Issue Series

Are Books Becoming Extinct?

Are Textbooks Biased?

Do Students Have Too Much Homework?

Standardized Testing

Student Loans

Current Controversies Series

America's Teachers

The Global Impact of Social Media

"Congress shall make
no law ... abridging
the freedom of speech,
or of the press."

First Amendment to the US Constitution

The basic foundation of our democracy is the First Amendment guarantee of freedom of expression. The Opposing Viewpoints series is dedicated to the concept of this basic freedom and the idea that it is more important to practice it than to enshrine it.

OPPOSING VIEWPOINTS® SERIES

Charter Schools

Margaret Haerens and Lynn M. Zott, Book Editors

WITHDRAWN

GREENHAVEN PRESS
A part of Gale, Cengage Learning

GALE
CENGAGE Learning·

Detroit • New York • San Francisco • New Haven, Conn • Waterville, Maine • London

Elizabeth Des Chenes, *Managing Editor*

© 2012 Greenhaven Press, a part of Gale, Cengage Learning.

Gale and Greenhaven Press are registered trademarks used herein under license.

For more information, contact:
Greenhaven Press
27500 Drake Rd.
Farmington Hills, MI 48331-3535
Or you can visit our Internet site at gale.cengage.com

Articles in Greenhaven Press anthologies are often edited for length to meet page requirements. In addition, original titles of these works are changed to clearly present the main thesis and to explicitly indicate the author's opinion. Every effort is made to ensure that Greenhaven Press accurately reflects the original intent of the authors. Every effort has been made to trace the owners of copyrighted material.

Cover Image copyright © David Hoare/Alamy.

LIBRARY OF CONGRESS CATALOGING-IN-PUBLICATION DATA

Charter Schools / Margaret Haerens, Lynn M. Zott, book editors.
    p. cm. -- (Opposing viewpoints)
    Includes bibliographical references and index.
    ISBN 978-0-7377-5442-1 (hardcover) -- ISBN 978-0-7377-5443-8 (pbk.)
    1. Charter schools--United States--Juvenile literature. I. I. Haerens, Margaret. II. Zott, Lynn M. (Lynn Marie), 1969-
    LB2806.36.C5354 2012
    371.050973--dc23

              2011029233

Printed in the United States of America
2 3 4 5 6   16 15 14 13 12
FD072

Contents

Chapter 3: Do Online Charter Schools Work?

Why Consider Opposing Viewpoints?

> *"The only way in which a human being can make some approach to knowing the whole of a subject is by hearing what can be said about it by persons of every variety of opinion and studying all modes in which it can be looked at by every character of mind. No wise man ever acquired his wisdom in any mode but this."*
>
> *John Stuart Mill*

In our media-intensive culture it is not difficult to find differing opinions. Thousands of newspapers and magazines and dozens of radio and television talk shows resound with differing points of view. The difficulty lies in deciding which opinion to agree with and which "experts" seem the most credible. The more inundated we become with differing opinions and claims, the more essential it is to hone critical reading and thinking skills to evaluate these ideas. Opposing Viewpoints books address this problem directly by presenting stimulating debates that can be used to enhance and teach these skills. The varied opinions contained in each book examine many different aspects of a single issue. While examining these conveniently edited opposing views, readers can develop critical thinking skills such as the ability to compare and contrast authors' credibility, facts, argumentation styles, use of persuasive techniques, and other stylistic tools. In short, the Opposing Viewpoints Series is an ideal way to attain the higher-level thinking and reading skills so essential in a culture of diverse and contradictory opinions.

In addition to providing a tool for critical thinking, Opposing Viewpoints books challenge readers to question their own strongly held opinions and assumptions. Most people form their opinions on the basis of upbringing, peer pressure, and personal, cultural, or professional bias. By reading carefully balanced opposing views, readers must directly confront new ideas as well as the opinions of those with whom they disagree. This is not to argue simplistically that everyone who reads opposing views will—or should—change his or her opinion. Instead, the series enhances readers' understanding of their own views by encouraging confrontation with opposing ideas. Careful examination of others' views can lead to the readers' understanding of the logical inconsistencies in their own opinions, perspective on why they hold an opinion, and the consideration of the possibility that their opinion requires further evaluation.

Evaluating Other Opinions

To ensure that this type of examination occurs, Opposing Viewpoints books present all types of opinions. Prominent spokespeople on different sides of each issue as well as well-known professionals from many disciplines challenge the reader. An additional goal of the series is to provide a forum for other, less known, or even unpopular viewpoints. The opinion of an ordinary person who has had to make the decision to cut off life support from a terminally ill relative, for example, may be just as valuable and provide just as much insight as a medical ethicist's professional opinion. The editors have two additional purposes in including these less known views. One, the editors encourage readers to respect others' opinions—even when not enhanced by professional credibility. It is only by reading or listening to and objectively evaluating others' ideas that one can determine whether they are worthy of consideration. Two, the inclusion of such viewpoints encourages the important critical thinking skill of objectively evaluating an author's credentials and bias. This evaluation will illuminate an author's reasons for taking a particular stance on an issue and will aid in readers' evaluation of the author's ideas.

It is our hope that these books will give readers a deeper understanding of the issues debated and an appreciation of the complexity of even seemingly simple issues when good and honest people disagree. This awareness is particularly important in a democratic society such as ours in which people enter into public debate to determine the common good. Those with whom one disagrees should not be regarded as enemies but rather as people whose views deserve careful examination and may shed light on one's own.

Thomas Jefferson once said that "difference of opinion leads to inquiry, and inquiry to truth." Jefferson, a broadly educated man, argued that "if a nation expects to be ignorant and free . . . it expects what never was and never will be." As individuals and as a nation, it is imperative that we consider the opinions of others and examine them with skill and discernment. The Opposing Viewpoints series is intended to help readers achieve this goal.

David L. Bender and Bruno Leone,
Founders

Introduction

> *"Some of the best ideas in education don't come from Washington, but from local schools all over America. That's why charter schools are a great way for us to learn from experiments in Topeka and Springfield that schools in Chicago and L.A. can replicate in their own class-rooms."*
>
> —Senator Barack Obama,
> March 8, 2005, remarks at TechNet

Since charter school laws were first passed in the early 1990s, charter schools have become a phenomenon in education. Charter schools are run independently from the traditional public school system and place an emphasis on innovation and curricula that are shaped to fit a community's needs. Supporters view charter schools as the key to increasing educational choice for students and parents and forcing innovation and competition within the public school system.

The history of charter schools can be traced back to education reformers looking for new ways to revitalize public education. In the 1960s and '70s educators all over the country were experimenting with alternative schools, public school choice, privatization, and community-parental empowerment. The concept of "charter" schools was devised by Ray Budde, an educator and administrator who became interested in organizational theory while teaching educational administration at the University of Massachusetts in the early 1970s. Budde suggested that education reform could be facilitated if groups of teachers were awarded contracts, or charters, by their local school boards to come up with new approaches tailored to the needs of their communities and students. These experiments would then be implemented within existing schools in the school districts. Budde presented his ideas on charter schools in "Education by Charter," a paper he presented in 1974 to the Society for General Systems Research.

At the time Budde's colleagues thought the idea of charters was too radical. As Budde recalled, no one thought the problems in education were so bad that they needed such extreme reform. So the idea lay dormant for years, until the movement for education reform gained steam in the mid-1980s. At that time, report after report denigrated the state of American education, contending that American students were being left behind in relation to other countries. Education reform became a pressing political and social issue.

Budde's paper on charter schools was published again in 1988, this time to a much more receptive audience. One of his supporters was Albert Shanker, the president of the American Federation of Teachers. Shanker expressed the union's support for Budde's charter school idea and expanded on it by calling for the creation of new schools based on the chartering concept. Instead of groups of teachers implementing limited charter programs within existing schools, the charter would extend to entire schools. With the growing support of unions, educators, and politicians, the charter school movement began to spread. In the late 1980s several charter programs were created in Philadelphia within existing schools.

Minnesota was the first state to fully envision and work toward a system of new charter schools. A study committee adopted the concept, devising a plan for charter schools based on three key values: opportunity, choice, and accountability. The state passed the first charter school law in 1991. A year later, California passed its own version. By 1995 nineteen states had passed laws that allowed charter schools. In 2009 there were forty-one. Charter schools are one of the fastest-growing innovations in education policy today.

The first charter school to open in the United States was the City Academy in St. Paul, Minnesota, which opened its doors on September 7, 1992. A number of others quickly followed, as states began to pass their own charter laws. Some focused on art, math or science; others on troubled students, such as dropouts, recovering drug addicts, or teen parents; others on disabled children with special needs. For parents and students who did not fit into traditional public schools or were in poorly performing school districts, charter schools presented a viable alternative to local public schools.

The growing popularity of charter schools received a tremendous boost from the US government in 2001 with the passage of No Child Left Behind, a law that called for expanded funding of charter schools and other alternative schooling. School choice became a political issue, as conservative politicians pushed for vouchers and charter schools to increase educational options for students and provide competition for traditional schools—a competition meant to spur innovation and achievement in both charters and traditional public schools. Recent presidents, including Bill Clinton, George W. Bush, and Barack Obama have all supported the charter school movement.

In recent years, however, a sharp backlash against charter schools has occurred. Many of the reformers who first saw charters as a welcome innovation now question the achievements of charters. One of those reformers is Diane Ravitch, former assistant secretary of education during the George H.W. Bush administration, who stated her change of heart in a March 2010 *Wall Street Journal* editorial:

> When charter schools started in the early 1990s, their supporters promised that they would unleash a new era of innovation and effectiveness. Now there are some 5,000 charter schools, which serve about 3% of the nation's students, and the Obama administration is pushing for many more. But the promise has not been fulfilled. Most studies of char-

ter schools acknowledge that they vary widely in quality. The only major national evaluation of charter schools was carried out by economist Margaret Raymond and funded by pro-charter foundations. Her group found that compared to regular public schools, 17% of charters got higher test scores, 46% had gains that were no different than their public counterparts, and 37% were significantly worse.

These statistics and other studies showing the mixed academic achievements of charter schools have generated a growing controversy over the charter school movement. This controversy is one of the key issues explored in this volume, *Opposing Viewpoints: Charter Schools*, which investigates the charter school movement in the following chapters: Are Charter Schools a Good Alternative to Public Schools?, Are Religious Charter Schools a Viable Choice?, Do Online Charter Schools Work?, and How Can Charter Schools Be Improved? The information in this volume will provide insight into the controversies surrounding online and religious charters and the academic achievement of charter schools.

OPPOSING
VIEWPOINTS®
SERIES

CHAPTER 1

Are Charter Schools a Good Alternative to Public Schools?

Chapter Preface

In 2008 a new charter school, the Science and Math Academy, opened in the city of New Orleans. Called the Sci Academy, the school is geared toward preparing ninth graders for a rigorous high school experience—and beyond that, college. Many Sci Academy students, however, were coming to the school with strikes against them. A fair percentage of them had missed significant schooling—up to a full school year—because of the destruction of their community by Hurricane Katrina in 2005 that set them back academically. More than half the students in the inaugural class had failed state promotional tests. Just as troubling, more than 70 percent read well below their grade level, with most below a fourth-grade reading level.

The educators and administrators of Sci Academy developed an academic program to address these deficits. They focused on not only bringing the students up to speed but also inspiring them to surpass expectations. That inaugural class, which had initially exhibited such troubling academic challenges, scored a 76 percent on Louisiana's state promotional test at the end of the year, making it the third most successful high school in New Orleans. In 2010 students at Sci Academy did even better: 80 percent passed the English section on the graduate exam, and 88 percent passed the math section. Sci Academy was acknowledged as such a success that it received a coveted $1 million grant from Oprah Winfrey's Angel Network, only one of six American schools to receive the honor.

Not many charter schools can boast of the amazing success that Sci Academy achieved in such a short time. In fact, for every success story, there is an example of charter school failure. Most studies of the movement acknowledge that charter schools vary widely in quality. One major study by economist Margaret Raymond evaluated the performance of charter schools at a national level and found that they didn't match up that well with traditional public schools: 17 percent of charters received higher test scores, 46 percent performed just as well as traditional public schools, and 37 percent tested significantly worse than their public school counterparts.

An example of the failure of charter schools is the Texans Can charter school chain. Texans Can operates ten charter schools in the state that are geared toward students with such challenges as teen parenthood, emotional issues, and drug addiction. In 2010 nine of the ten schools operated by Texans Can were rated "academically unacceptable" by the state. Schools repeatedly violated academic standards, which prompted the state to threaten to close three of the schools. At one of the troubled schools, not one of the fifteen freshmen enrolled in 2001–02 managed to earn a high school diploma within six years.

Despite its poor academic record, the Texans Can company continues to receive public money. The state allocates $32 million to the schools each year, and Texans Can raises another $8 million. Moreover, Texans Can executives continue to receive generous paychecks—the top six executives earn a combined $880,000—while the students continue to struggle academically.

The Sci Academy in New Orleans and the Texans Can charter schools in Texas are just two examples of the impressive successes and the abysmal failures of the charter school movement in the United States. The question of whether charter schools are a viable alternative to traditional public schools is explored in the following chapter, which considers the overall success of the charter school movement, as well as the role of charter schools in American education.

> *"Public charter schools are simply an-*
> *other way to give parents choices in*
> *education for their children."*

Charter Schools Are Superior to Public Schools

Ben Adams

Ben Adams is the cofounder of West Virginians for Education Reform. In the following viewpoint, he advocates for the reform of West Virginia's school system, particularly favoring the passage of a law allowing charter schools in the state. Adams notes that in recent rankings from Newsweek, *a high percentage of charter schools were classified among the best public high schools in the country, indicating that charter schools are doing an excellent job educating young students. He argues that West Virginia needs such schools, and parents need the choice of innovative, independent charter schools for their children.*

As you read, consider the following questions:

1. According to the author, how many public charter schools made *Newsweek*'s 2010 top public high schools in America list?

2. How much higher are graduation rates of charter schools than traditional public schools, according to a RAND study?

3. How many states currently prohibit charter schools, according to Adams?

Each year, *Newsweek* chooses the best public high schools in the country based on how hard schools work to challenge students with advanced-placement, college-level courses and tests.

For 2010, just over 1,600 schools—or 6 percent of all the public schools in the United States—made the list.

What's notable is that 15 public charter schools made the Top 100 list, though charters only represent 5 percent of all high schools. Thirteen of the charter high schools were start-up schools [schools started from scratch], while only two were conversions from traditional public schools.

Sadly, not one single public high school from West Virginia made the Top 100 list.

In fact, West Virginia had just four schools even make the overall list of the top 1,623 schools. The state's highest-ranked school, George Washington High School in Charleston, also our only high school in the top 1,000, came in at only No. 678.

The Educational System in West Virginia

As cofounder of West Virginians for Education Reform, and as a recent graduate of the state's public school system, I remind citizens and lawmakers that our state ranks 50th in the nation in the number of adults with bachelor's degrees, and that recent survey results show that 86 percent of West Virginia residents favor more public school options.

To me, both data points provide an overwhelming message from parents, business and community members, as well as taxpayers and citizens, that it is time our state creates and

What Are Charter Schools?

A charter school is a publicly funded school that is typically governed by a group or organization under a legislative contract or charter with the state; the charter exempts the school from selected state or local rules and regulations. In return for funding and autonomy, the charter school must meet the accountability standards articulated in its charter. A school's charter is reviewed periodically (typically every 3 to 5 years) and can be revoked if guidelines on curriculum and management are not followed or the standards are not met. As of February 2010, charter schools operate in 40 states and the District of Columbia. In the following states, a charter school law has not been passed: Alabama, Kentucky, Maine, Montana, Nebraska, North Dakota, South Dakota, Vermont, Washington, and West Virginia.

"The Condition of Education 2010,"
US Department of Education, 2010.

passes a comprehensive state charter law that will explicitly allow for start-up public charter schools.

With our graduation rate recently calculated at 71 percent, it is very clear that we are not doing the job of preparing over a quarter of a million of our public school students for college and beyond. The time for real reform is now.

School Choice Is Key

West Virginians want more public school choices, including charter schools—independent, innovative public schools that are held accountable for improved student achievement.

A recent RAND study [a study conducted by the RAND Corporation, a public policy think tank] shows that charter schools have graduation rates 7 percent to 15 percent higher than traditional public schools. In addition, in Chicago and Florida, students in charter high schools benefited from an 8 to 10 percentage point increase in their likelihood to attend college.

Yet, despite such positive data, West Virginia is one of only 10 states that currently prohibits charter schools.

This year [2010], state lawmakers have made great strides to introduce charter school legislation. However, it includes restrictions that have proven ineffective in other states, such as not explicitly allowing for start-up charter schools.

By not explicitly allowing these schools to be started from scratch, we are severely limiting the ability of educators and community groups to create schools of excellence that will prepare students for college and the workforce. At the end of the day, families in West Virginia are left with only two choices—traditional public schools and private schools for those families who can afford them.

Charter School Stereotypes

It is often thought that charter schools are an "urban solution" that is most effective and successful in inner cities with high minority and poverty levels, but that is simply not true.

Take BASIS charter high school in Tucson, Ariz., for example. It is one of the top-ranked public charter schools on *Newsweek*'s list at No. 6.

It is a start-up charter school that began in 1997 when economists Michael and Olga Block set out to create a model. The result of their vision has received consistent national praise and attention, with 100 percent of their students meeting or exceeding state standards on all subjects of the state's high school exit exams and moving on to college.

Northcoast Preparatory, in rural Areata, Calif., came in at No. 23 on *Newsweek*'s list.

Opened as a start-up charter school in 2000, this unique high school is based on the International Baccalaureate model and stresses critical thinking, performing and fine arts, community service and international travel—all while providing their students with university-level academic courses.

The Search for Opportunity

The bottom line is that our education system in West Virginia is struggling. We are consistently ranked at the bottom of lists that we don't want to be on, and rarely make an appearance on the top lists in education.

President John F. Kennedy said that "all of us do not have equal talent, but all of us should have an equal opportunity to develop our talent."

Public charter schools are simply another way to give parents choices in education for their children. The students in this state deserve every opportunity to have an exceptional education that will prepare them for success in our global economy.

> "Both in Indianapolis and nationally, charters—just like regular public schools—can't be successful without attracting and maintaining a steady stream of good leaders and teachers."

Charter Schools Have Had Mixed Results

Sarah Butrymowicz

Sarah Butrymowicz is a writer for the Hechinger Report *and was a contributor to the Politics Daily website. In the following viewpoint, she maintains that although charter schools have been extremely popular in states like Indiana, they have had mixed results. Butrymowicz notes that although policy makers and educators have had high hopes for charters, the schools often strongly resemble traditional public schools in that they have trouble innovating and attracting high-quality teachers and administrators. For many charters, Butrymowicz reports, it is very difficult to replicate the success of the best charter schools, as experiences in Indianapolis show.*

As you read, consider the following questions:

1. According to the Center on Reinventing Public Education, how many charter schools are there in the United States?

2. According to the viewpoint author, why did charter schools become popular with conservatives and become criticized by former supporters?

3. What percentage of Indiana schoolkids attend charter schools, according to the author?

Principal Marcus Robinson strides down the hallway of Indianapolis's Charles A. Tindley Accelerated School, past a wall that proclaims in huge letters "COLLEGE OR DIE." His maroon polo shirt and khakis match the uniforms of middle schoolers standing in line for the bathroom, their noses buried in books.

In a booming voice, Robinson praises them for their diligence then continues with his rounds. He picks up pieces of trash, chastises students who are talking as they switch rooms, and singles out a girl for being too loud, telling her, "I need your leadership." Robinson's tough-love, no-excuses approach is getting results: The average sixth grader enters performing well below grade level. By the time they graduate from high school, Tindley's students will be among the highest performing in the city. All will have taken some college courses and been admitted to four-year colleges.

A Success Story

As a charter school, Tindley operates independently of the city's public school districts and offers what charter advocates say is a better public alternative for disadvantaged students. Some 2,100 Indianapolis students are on waiting lists to get into charter schools, even though not all are doing as well as Tindley.

Tindley's success comes as Mitch Daniels, the Republican governor of Indiana and a potential 2012 presidential contender, is pushing for far more charters in the state, and as the Indiana House is poised to vote on a new charter expansion law.

Along with newly elected Republican governors in Florida, Nevada and Wisconsin, Daniels is also advocating taxpayer-financed vouchers to send children to private schools. While voucher plans have faced fierce opposition from teachers' unions and many Democratic politicians, it is Daniels's charter school agenda that puts him on rare common ground with President [Barack] Obama, who has enticed states with federal money to increase the number of charter schools nationwide.

Since 2009, when Obama first introduced the competitive grant program known as Race to the Top, 14 states have eased their restrictions on the number of charters permitted. "Charter schools aren't a magic bullet, but I want to give states and school districts the chance to try new things," Obama said last July [2010]. "If a charter school works, then let's apply those lessons elsewhere."

The Truth About Charters

Policy makers and reformers on both sides of the aisle have long touted charter schools as a way to improve all schools, and charters are indeed booming. There are about 4,900 charter schools in the United States, and on average 400 new charters open every year, according to the Center on Reinventing Public Education at the University of Washington Bothell.

At the same time, anecdotal evidence and research from around the country suggest that charters, which still enroll only about 3 percent of all U.S. students, don't necessarily spur other public schools to improve. Indianapolis, which is known for having some of the worst public school districts in the country, provides a perfect example of how complex the notion can be.

"The thought was that 'a higher tide raises all boats,'" said David Harris, who served as former Indianapolis Mayor Bart Peterson's right-hand man when the city's charter movement began nine years ago. "It's been a disappointment both in Indianapolis and around the country," Harris said.

As Daniels advocates charter expansion in Indiana and Obama promotes charters-as-laboratories across the country, Indianapolis shows there's good reason to be wary of politicians' claims that charters can improve the quality of education for students in all public schools. Even charter operators have moved away from promoting charters as the saviors of public education.

History of Charters

The notion that charters will have influence beyond their walls—whether through cooperation or competition—has been around for decades and has received support from many political camps. Even Albert Shanker, the liberal former president of the American Federation of Teachers, thought charter schools would encourage innovative ways of educating when the concept was introduced in the late 1980s.

By the 1990s, charters became the preferred school-choice option for conservative reformers because vouchers were seen as too divisive. Advocates believed that by introducing competition, public schools afraid of losing students and money would be spurred to step up their own performance. As this line of thinking took hold, Shanker morphed into an outspoken critic of charter schools.

Indianapolis launched its own charter experiment after the state passed a law in 2001 that gave Indianapolis's mayor the power to authorize charter schools within city limits. It remains the only law of its kind nationwide, and it was launched partly in the hope that spurring competition would improve all schools.

At the time, the Indianapolis Public Schools (IPS), the largest of 11 school districts in the city, had a graduation rate of about 30 percent, along with test scores that fell well below the state average. The district has since opened a number of magnet schools in response to the mayor's charter schools, and it has made some strides in recent years. But the district's graduation rate still hovers around 50 percent, and test scores, although higher, are still far below state average. Only 28 out of 77 IPS schools met federal adequate yearly progress (AYP) requirements last year, and there's no clear way to attribute any of IPS's successes or failures to charter schools.

There are some indications, though, of where charters fall short. For instance, only 6 out of 15 met AYP in 2008–2009— roughly the same percentage as in IPS. The mayor's charter team, however, found that 61 percent of charter school students were proficient in English last year and 64 percent were in math, compared to 54 percent and 58 percent, respectively, at the schools these students would have attended if the charters didn't exist.

Different Rules

Eugene White, the superintendent of IPS, isn't against charter schools but says he can't compete anymore because he is "bleeding students" to them. As a result, he's lobbied the state for a charter cap, and spoke out against Daniels's plan last week.

In Indianapolis, students have flocked to charters. Some 8,400 students now attend charter schools authorized by the mayor, while an additional 1,650 students attend charters authorized by Ball State University in Indianapolis. In all, close to 6 percent of the city's students go to charters.

Last year, about 70 percent of charter school students lived within the IPS attendance zone. But Karega Rausch, director of the Office of Education Innovation in Indianapolis, said 65.3 percent of students who have left IPS in the last four years actually switched to a school in one of the 10 other districts within the city. IPS has lost an average of 1,200 students annually over the past three years, although that number is declining.

Reform Is Difficult

Losing students to charters is not the only thing that has held IPS back from making sweeping changes, though. As Rausch put it: "Reforming traditional districts is like turning the *Titanic* around."

Union contracts provide a case in point. Poorly performing teachers aren't easy to get rid of in most public schools. This isn't true at charters, though. For instance, when the Tindley Academy hit a rough spot early on, Robinson, the principal, held a meeting with teachers about how to improve student performance. A number of teachers favored creating a "Tindley-lite" track for those not capable of reaching the school's high standards. Robinson says he fired everyone who advocated that approach.

Tindley teachers, like many who work in charter schools, also work long hours: from 8 A.M. to 5 P.M. during the school year, as well as additional hours over the summer. It's a different story in traditional public schools. Teachers' contracts in Indiana spell out how many hours teachers work and how they can be terminated. "We have a whole process we have to go through," White said.

Missing the Boat

Charter school principal Carey Dahncke has taken full advantage of the new freedom he now has. Since leaving his position as principal of an IPS elementary school in 2006 to take over the K–9 Christel House Academy, Dahncke has been able to partner with health organizations on wellness initiatives, local colleges to teach music lessons and an outdoor group to take students on yearly camping trips.

"Here we're a lot more innovative because we can be," he said, noting how decisions that can take years to make in the public school world can be made almost instantly at Christel House.

But that doesn't mean he feels the success of his school—one of the highest-performing in Indianapolis—can be copied in a "cookie-cutter" way. And he doesn't specifically work with IPS schools to share his model or insights with them.

In Indianapolis, some of the mayor's charter schools have a unique spin to them. For instance, one charter is specifically for students who have dropped out and another caters to students with substance abuse problems. Still, White, the IPS superintendent, isn't impressed with the innovation of charter schools in the city, and he doesn't think there'd be much to learn if they were to collaborate. With few exceptions, he said, these charters mimic programs his district already has. "Charters have missed the boat somewhat," he said.

Innovation in Charter Schools

His critique is one heard around the country as charters began to grow in earnest. "It became very clear that charters on the whole are not as innovative as a lot of people would like them to be," said Jeffrey Henig, a professor of education at Columbia University's Teachers College. Other than lengthening the school day and year—which can be politically difficult to do in regular school districts—many charters still resemble traditional public schools.

Harris, who now heads the nonprofit Mind Trust in Indianapolis, believes that replicating success in charters won't get easier, regardless of how creative they are. Both in Indianapolis and nationally, charters—just like regular public schools—can't be successful without attracting and maintaining a steady stream of good leaders and teachers.

"What makes charter schools great aren't specific best practices as much as empowering really talented people to do really innovative things," said Harris. "This 'best practices' view of the world—it's limited by who is doing the replication of the best practices."

> "There was a time—which now seems distant—when most people assumed that students' performance in school was largely determined by their own efforts and by the circumstances and support of their family, not by their teachers."

The Success of Charter Schools Is a Myth

Diane Ravitch

Diane Ravitch is a research professor of education at New York University, a nonresident senior fellow at the Brookings Institution, the former assistant secretary of education during the George H.W. Bush administration, and the author of The Death and Life of the Great American School System: How Testing and Choice Are Undermining Education. *In the following viewpoint, she points out that a slew of recent documentaries, including the popular* Waiting for "Superman," *unfairly blame public schools, teachers, and unions for the prevailing public feeling that our society is falling behind in a global marketplace. Ravitch excoriates the films for their simplistic, misleading, and of-*

Diane Ravitch, "The Myth of Charter Schools," *New York Review of Books*, November 11, 2010. Copyright © New York Review of Books. All rights reserved. Reproduced by permission.

ten inaccurate messages about education, noting that they fail to present the true state of charter schools—that they are often mismanaged and expensive failures, no better than traditional public schools, and function as a tool for political interests to privatize education. Ravitch underscores the importance of nonschool factors—poverty, nutrition, parental neglect, and health—that play a bigger role in student achievement than teacher quality and concludes that charter schools are not the cure-all that some educational reformers would have the public believe.

As you read, consider the following questions:

1. According to a Gallup poll, what percentage of American parents awarded their child's public school a grade of A or B?

2. According to the CREDO study cited by Ravitch, how many of five charter schools are able to achieve the "amazing results" celebrated in the film *Waiting for "Superman"*?

3. What percentage of achievement is determined by factors not related to school, according to economist Dan Goldhaber?

Ordinarily, documentaries about education attract little attention, and seldom, if ever, reach neighborhood movie theaters. Davis Guggenheim's *Waiting for "Superman"* is different. It arrived in late September with the biggest publicity splash I have ever seen for a documentary. Not only was it the subject of major stories in *Time* and *New York*, but it was featured twice on *The Oprah Winfrey Show* and was the centerpiece of several days of programming by NBC, including an interview with President Obama.

Two other films expounding the same arguments—*The Lottery* and *The Cartel*—were released in the late spring, but they received far less attention than Guggenheim's film. His reputation as the director of the Academy Award–winning *An*

Inconvenient Truth, about global warming, contributed to the anticipation surrounding *Waiting for "Superman,"* but the media frenzy suggested something more. Guggenheim presents the popularized version of an account of American public education that is promoted by some of the nation's most powerful figures and institutions.

The message of these films has become alarmingly familiar: American public education is a failed enterprise. The problem is not money. Public schools already spend too much. Test scores are low because there are so many bad teachers, whose jobs are protected by powerful unions. Students drop out because the schools fail them, but they could accomplish practically anything if they were saved from bad teachers. They would get higher test scores if schools could fire more bad teachers and pay more to good ones. The only hope for the future of our society, especially for poor black and Hispanic children, is escape from public schools, especially to charter schools, which are mostly funded by the government but controlled by private organizations, many of them operating to make a profit.

The Cartel maintains that we must not only create more charter schools, but provide vouchers so that children can flee incompetent public schools and attend private schools. There, we are led to believe, teachers will be caring and highly skilled (unlike the lazy dullards in public schools); the schools will have high expectations and test scores will soar; and all children will succeed academically, regardless of their circumstances. *The Lottery* echoes the main story line of *Waiting for "Superman"*: It is about children who are desperate to avoid the New York City public schools and eager to win a spot in a shiny new charter school in Harlem.

For many people, these arguments require a willing suspension of disbelief. Most Americans graduated from public schools, and most went from school to college or the workplace without thinking that their school had limited their life chances. There was a time—which now seems distant—when most people assumed that students' performance in school was largely determined by their own efforts and by the circumstances and support of their family, not by their teachers. There were good teachers and mediocre teachers, even bad teachers, but in the end, most public schools offered ample opportunity for education to those willing to pursue it. The annual Gallup poll about education shows that Americans are overwhelmingly dissatisfied with the quality of the nation's schools, but 77 percent of public school parents award their own child's public school a grade of A or B, the highest level of approval since the question was first asked in 1985.

Waiting for "Superman" and the other films appeal to a broad apprehension that the nation is falling behind in global competition. If the economy is a shambles, if poverty persists for significant segments of the population, if American kids are not as serious about their studies as their peers in other nations, the schools must be to blame. At last we have the culprit on which we can pin our anger, our palpable sense that something is very wrong with our society, that we are on the wrong track, and that America is losing the race for global dominance. It is not globalization or deindustrialization or poverty or our coarse popular culture or predatory financial practices that bear responsibility: It's the public schools, their teachers, and their unions.

The inspiration for *Waiting for "Superman"* began, Guggenheim explains, as he drove his own children to a private school, past the neighborhood schools with low test scores. He wondered about the fate of the children whose families did not have the choice of schools available to his own children. What was the quality of their education? He was sure it must be terrible. The press release for the film says that he wondered, "How heartsick and worried did *their* parents feel as they dropped their kids off this morning?" Guggenheim is a graduate of Sidwell Friends, the elite private school in Washington,

D.C., where President Obama's daughters are enrolled. The public schools that he passed by each morning must have seemed as hopeless and dreadful to him as the public schools in Washington that his own parents had shunned.

Waiting for "Superman" tells the story of five children who enter a lottery to win a coveted place in a charter school. Four of them seek to escape the public schools; one was asked to leave a Catholic school because her mother couldn't afford the tuition. Four of the children are black or Hispanic and live in gritty neighborhoods, while the one white child lives in a leafy suburb. We come to know each of these children and their families; we learn about their dreams for the future; we see that they are lovable; and we identify with them. By the end of the film, we are rooting for them as the day of the lottery approaches.

In each of the schools to which they have applied, the odds against them are large. Anthony, a fifth grader in Washington, D.C., applies to the SEED charter boarding school, where there are sixty-one applicants for twenty-four places. Francisco is a first-grade student in the Bronx whose mother (a social worker with a graduate degree) is desperate to get him out of the New York City public schools and into a charter school; she applies to Harlem Success Academy where he is one of 792 applicants for forty places. Bianca is the kindergarten student in Harlem whose mother cannot afford Catholic school tuition; she enters the lottery at another Harlem Success Academy, as one of 767 students competing for thirty-five openings. Daisy is a fifth-grade student in East Los Angeles whose parents hope she can win a spot at KIPP LA Prep, where 135 students have applied for ten places. Emily is an eighth-grade student in Silicon Valley, where the local high school has gorgeous facilities, high graduation rates, and impressive test scores, but her family worries that she will be assigned to a slow track because of her low test scores; so they enter the lottery for Summit Preparatory Charter High School, where she is one of 455 students competing for 110 places.

The stars of the film are Geoffrey Canada, the CEO of the Harlem Children's Zone, which provides a broad variety of social services to families and children and runs two charter schools; Michelle Rhee, chancellor of the Washington, D.C., public school system, who closed schools, fired teachers and principals, and gained a national reputation for her tough policies; David Levin and Michael Feinberg, who have built a network of nearly one hundred high-performing KIPP charter schools over the past sixteen years; and Randi Weingarten, president of the American Federation of Teachers, who is cast in the role of chief villain. Other charter school leaders, like Steve Barr of the Green Dot chain in Los Angeles, do star turns, as does Bill Gates of Microsoft, whose foundation has invested many millions of dollars in expanding the number of charter schools. No successful public school teacher or principal or superintendent appears in the film; indeed there is no mention of any successful public school, only the incessant drumbeat on the theme of public school failure.

The situation is dire, the film warns us. We must act. But what must we do? The message of the film is clear. Public schools are bad, privately managed charter schools are good. Parents clamor to get their children out of the public schools in New York City (despite the claims by Mayor Michael Bloomberg that the city's schools are better than ever) and into the charters (the mayor also plans to double the number of charters, to help more families escape from the public schools that he controls). If we could fire the bottom 5 to 10 percent of the lowest-performing teachers every year, says Hoover Institution economist Eric Hanushek in the film, our national test scores would soon approach the top of international rankings in mathematics and science.

Some fact-checking is in order, and the place to start is with the film's quiet acknowledgment that only one in five

"*I thought you said charter schools were going to solve all our problems? But their test scores are worse than the public schools!*"
"*That's because charter schools get all the poor kids and the disciplinary problems and the demanding parents.*"

Copyright © FNO Press; Excuses, Excuses, Excuses by Jerry King. nochildleft.com.

charter schools is able to get the "amazing results" that it celebrates. Nothing more is said about this astonishing statistic. It is drawn from a national study of charter schools by Stanford economist Margaret Raymond (the wife of Hanushek). Known as the CREDO study, it evaluated student progress on math tests in half the nation's five thousand charter schools and concluded that 17 percent were superior to a matched traditional public school; 37 percent were worse than the public school; and the remaining 46 percent had academic gains no different from that of a similar public school. The proportion of charters that get amazing results is far smaller than 17 percent. Why did Davis Guggenheim pay no attention to the charter schools that are run by incompetent leaders or corporations mainly concerned to make money? Why propound to an unknowing public the myth that charter schools are the answer to our educational woes, when the filmmaker knows that there are twice as many failing charters as there are successful ones? Why not give an honest accounting?

The propagandistic nature of *Waiting for "Superman"* is revealed by Guggenheim's complete indifference to the wide variation among charter schools. There are excellent charter schools, just as there are excellent public schools. Why did he not also inquire into the charter chains that are mired in unsavory real estate deals, or take his camera to the charters where most students are getting lower scores than those in the neighborhood public schools? Why did he not report on the charter principals who have been indicted for embezzlement, or the charters that blur the line between church and state? Why did he not look into the charter schools whose leaders are paid $300,000–$400,000 a year to oversee small numbers of schools and students?

Guggenheim seems to believe that teachers alone can overcome the effects of student poverty, even though there are countless studies that demonstrate the link between income and test scores. He shows us footage of the pilot Chuck Yeager breaking the sound barrier, to the amazement of people who said it couldn't be done. Since Yeager broke the sound barrier, we should be prepared to believe that able teachers are all it takes to overcome the disadvantages of poverty, homelessness, joblessness, poor nutrition, absent parents, etc.

The movie asserts a central thesis in today's school reform discussion: the idea that teachers are the most important factor determining student achievement. But this proposition is false. Hanushek has released studies showing that teacher quality accounts for about 7.5–10 percent of student test score gains. Several other high-quality analyses echo this finding, and while estimates vary a bit, there is a relative consensus: Teachers statistically account for around 10–20 percent of achievement outcomes. Teachers are the most important factor within schools.

But the same body of research shows that nonschool factors matter even more than teachers. According to University of Washington economist Dan Goldhaber, about 60 percent of achievement is explained by nonschool factors, such as family income. So while teachers are the most important factor within schools, their effects pale in comparison with those of students' backgrounds, families, and other factors beyond the control of schools and teachers. Teachers can have a profound effect on students, but it would be foolish to believe that teachers alone can undo the damage caused by poverty and its associated burdens.

Guggenheim skirts the issue of poverty by showing only families that are intact and dedicated to helping their children succeed. One of the children he follows is raised by a doting grandmother; two have single mothers who are relentless in seeking better education for them; two of them live with a mother and father. Nothing is said about children whose families are not available, for whatever reason, to support them, or about children who are homeless, or children with special needs. Nor is there any reference to the many charter schools that enroll disproportionately small numbers of children who are English-language learners or have disabilities.

The film never acknowledges that charter schools were created mainly at the instigation of Albert Shanker, the president of the American Federation of Teachers from 1974 to 1997. Shanker had the idea in 1988 that a group of public school teachers would ask their colleagues for permission to create a small school that would focus on the neediest students, those who had dropped out and those who were disengaged from school and likely to drop out. He sold the idea as a way to open schools that would collaborate with public schools and help motivate disengaged students. In 1993, Shanker turned against the charter school idea when he realized that for-profit organizations saw it as a business opportunity and were advancing an agenda of school privatization. Michelle Rhee gained her teaching experience in Baltimore as an employee of Education Alternatives, Inc., one of the first of the for-profit operations.

Today, charter schools are promoted not as ways to collaborate with public schools but as competitors that will force them to get better or go out of business. In fact, they have become the force for privatization that Shanker feared. Because of the high-stakes testing regime created by President George W. Bush's No Child Left Behind (NCLB) legislation, charter schools compete to get higher test scores than regular public schools and thus have an incentive to avoid students who might pull down their scores. Under NCLB, low-performing schools may be closed, while high-performing ones may get bonuses. Some charter schools "counsel out" or expel students just before state testing day. Some have high attrition rates, especially among lower-performing students.

Perhaps the greatest distortion in this film is its misrepresentation of data about student academic performance. The film claims that 70 percent of eighth-grade students cannot read at grade level. This is flatly wrong. Guggenheim here relies on numbers drawn from the federally sponsored National Assessment of Educational Progress (NAEP). I served as a member of the governing board for the national tests for seven years, and I know how misleading Guggenheim's figures are. NAEP doesn't measure performance in terms of grade-level achievement. The highest level of performance, "advanced," is equivalent to an A+, representing the highest possible academic performance. The next level, "proficient," is equivalent to an A or a very strong B. The next level is "basic," which probably translates into a C grade. The film assumes that any student below proficient is "below grade level." But it would be far more fitting to worry about students who are "below basic," who are 25 percent of the national sample, not 70 percent.

Guggenheim didn't bother to take a close look at the heroes of his documentary. Geoffrey Canada is justly celebrated for the creation of the Harlem Children's Zone, which not only runs two charter schools but surrounds children and their families with a broad array of social and medical services. Canada has a board of wealthy philanthropists and a very successful fund-raising apparatus. With assets of more than $200 million, his organization has no shortage of funds. Canada himself is currently paid $400,000 annually. For Guggenheim to praise Canada while also claiming that public schools don't need any more money is bizarre. Canada's charter schools get better results than nearby public schools serving impoverished students. If all inner-city schools had the same resources as his, they might get the same good results.

But contrary to the myth that Guggenheim propounds about "amazing results," even Geoffrey Canada's schools have many students who are not proficient. On the 2010 state tests, 60 percent of the fourth-grade students in one of his charter schools were not proficient in reading, nor were 50 percent in the other. It should be noted—and Guggenheim didn't note it—that Canada kicked out his entire first class of middle school students when they didn't get good enough test scores to satisfy his board of trustees. This sad event was documented by Paul Tough in his laudatory account of Canada's Harlem Children's Zone, *Whatever It Takes* (2009). Contrary to Guggenheim's mythology, even the best-funded charters, with the finest services, can't completely negate the effects of poverty.

Guggenheim ignored other clues that might have gotten in the way of a good story. While blasting the teachers' unions, he points to Finland as a nation whose educational system the US should emulate, not bothering to explain that it has a completely unionized teaching force. His documentary showers praise on testing and accountability, yet he does not acknowledge that Finland seldom tests its students. Any Finnish educator will say that Finland improved its public education system not by privatizing its schools or constantly testing its students, but by investing in the preparation, support, and retention of excellent teachers. It achieved its present eminence not by systematically firing 5–10 percent of its teachers, but by patiently building for the future. Finland has a national curriculum, which is not restricted to the basic skills of reading and math, but includes the arts, sciences, history, foreign languages, and other subjects that are essential to a good, rounded education. Finland also strengthened its social welfare programs for children and families. Guggenheim simply ignores the realities of the Finnish system.

In any school reform proposal, the question of "scalability" always arises. Can reforms be reproduced on a broad scale? The fact that one school produces amazing results is not in itself a demonstration that every other school can do the same. For example, Guggenheim holds up Locke High School in Los Angeles, part of the Green Dot charter chain, as a success story but does not tell the whole story. With an infusion of $15 million of mostly private funding, Green Dot produced a safer, cleaner campus, but no more than tiny improvements in its students' abysmal test scores. According to the *Los Angeles Times*, the percentage of its students proficient in English rose from 13.7 percent in 2009 to 14.9 percent in 2010, while in math the proportion of proficient students grew from 4 percent to 6.7 percent. What can be learned from this small progress? Becoming a charter is no guarantee that a school serving a tough neighborhood will produce educational miracles.

Another highly praised school that is featured in the film is the SEED charter boarding school in Washington, D.C. SEED seems to deserve all the praise that it receives from Guggenheim, CBS's *60 Minutes,* and elsewhere. It has remarkable rates of graduation and college acceptance. But SEED spends $35,000 per student, as compared to average current spending for public schools of about one-third that amount. Is our society prepared to open boarding schools for tens of thousands of inner-city students and pay what it costs to copy the SEED model? Those who claim that better education for the neediest students won't require more money cannot use SEED to support their argument.

Guggenheim seems to demand that public schools start firing "bad" teachers so they can get the great results that one of every five charter schools gets. But he never explains how difficult it is to identify "bad" teachers. If one looks only at test scores, teachers in affluent suburbs get higher ones. If one uses student gains or losses as a general measure, then those who teach the neediest children—English-language learners, troubled students, autistic students—will see the smallest gains, and teachers will have an incentive to avoid districts and classes with large numbers of the neediest students.

Ultimately the job of hiring teachers, evaluating them, and deciding who should stay and who should go falls to administrators. We should be taking a close look at those who award due process rights (the accurate term for "tenure") to too many incompetent teachers. The best way to ensure that there are no bad or ineffective teachers in our public schools is to insist that we have principals and supervisors who are knowledgeable and experienced educators. Yet there is currently a vogue to recruit and train principals who have little or no education experience. (The George W. Bush Institute just announced its intention to train 50,000 new principals in the next decade and to recruit non-educators for this sensitive post.)

Waiting for "Superman" is the most important public-relations coup that the critics of public education have made so far. Their power is not to be underestimated. For years, right-wing critics demanded vouchers and got nowhere. Now, many of them are watching in amazement as their ineffectual attacks on "government schools" and their advocacy of privately managed schools with public funding have become the received wisdom among liberal elites. Despite their uneven record, charter schools have the enthusiastic endorsement of the Obama administration, the Gates Foundation, the Broad Foundation, and the Dell Foundation. In recent months, the *New York Times* has published three stories about how charter schools have become the favorite cause of hedge fund executives. According to the *Times*, when Andrew Cuomo wanted to tap into Wall Street money for his gubernatorial campaign, he had to meet with the executive director of Democrats for Education Reform (DFER), a pro-charter group.

Dominated by hedge fund managers who control billions of dollars, DFER has contributed heavily to political candidates for local and state offices who pledge to promote charter schools. (Its efforts to unseat incumbents in three predominantly black State Senate districts in New York City came to nothing; none of its handpicked candidates received as much as 30 percent of the vote in the primary elections, even with the full-throated endorsement of the city's tabloids.) Despite the loss of local elections and the defeat of Washington, D.C., mayor Adrian Fenty (who had appointed the controversial schools chancellor Michelle Rhee), the combined clout of these groups, plus the enormous power of the federal government and the uncritical support of the major media, presents a serious challenge to the viability and future of public education.

It bears mentioning that nations with high-performing school systems—whether Korea, Singapore, Finland, or Japan—have succeeded not by privatizing their schools or closing those with low scores, but by strengthening the education profession. They also have less poverty than we do. Fewer than 5 percent of children in Finland live in poverty, as compared to 20 percent in the United States. Those who insist that poverty doesn't matter, that only teachers matter, prefer to ignore such contrasts.

If we are serious about improving our schools, we will take steps to improve our teacher force, as Finland and other nations have done. That would mean better screening to select the best candidates, higher salaries, better support and mentoring systems, and better working conditions. Guggenheim complains that only one in 2,500 teachers loses his or her teaching certificate, but fails to mention that 50 percent of those who enter teaching leave within five years, mostly because of poor working conditions, lack of adequate resources, and the stress of dealing with difficult children and disrespectful parents. Some who leave "fire themselves"; others were fired before they got tenure. We should also insist that only highly experienced teachers become principals (the "head teacher" in the school), not retired businessmen and military personnel. Every school should have a curriculum that includes a full range of studies, not just basic skills. And if we really are intent on school improvement, we must reduce the appalling rates of child poverty that impede success in school and in life.

There is a clash of ideas occurring in education right now between those who believe that public education is not only a fundamental right but a vital public service, akin to the public provision of police, fire protection, parks, and public libraries, and those who believe that the private sector is always superior to the public sector. *Waiting for "Superman"* is a powerful weapon on behalf of those championing the "free market" and privatization. It raises important questions, but all of the answers it offers require a transfer of public funds to the private sector. The stock market crash of 2008 should suffice to remind us that the managers of the private sector do not have a monopoly on success.

Public education is one of the cornerstones of American democracy. The public schools must accept everyone who appears at their doors, no matter their race, language, economic status, or disability. Like the huddled masses who arrived from Europe in years gone by, immigrants from across the world today turn to the public schools to learn what they need to know to become part of this society. The schools should be far better than they are now, but privatizing them is no solution.

In the final moments of *Waiting for "Superman,"* the children and their parents assemble in auditoriums in New York City, Washington, D.C., Los Angeles, and Silicon Valley, waiting nervously to see if they will win the lottery. As the camera pans the room, you see tears rolling down the cheeks of children and adults alike, all their hopes focused on a listing of numbers or names. Many people react to the scene with their own tears, sad for the children who lose. I had a different reaction. First, I thought to myself that the charter operators were cynically using children as political pawns in their own campaign to promote their cause. (Gail Collins in the *New York Times* had a similar reaction and wondered why they couldn't just send the families a letter in the mail instead of subjecting them to public rejection.) Second, I felt an immense sense of gratitude to the much-maligned American public education system, where no one has to win a lottery to gain admission.

> "Replacing the ossified monopoly system of assigned government schooling with a competitive, diversified education marketplace would introduce powerful incentives for all schools to perform."

Charters Will Raise the Quality of Traditional Public Schools

Vicki E. Murray

Vicki E. Murray is a senior fellow in education studies at the Pacific Research Institute and the co-author of Not as Good as You Think: Why the Middle Class Needs School Choice. *In the following viewpoint, she maintains that charter schools provide a healthy competition for traditional public schools, forcing them to improve the quality of education that they provide to students and improving test scores for reading and math. Murray argues that studies show that if American students were allowed to choose the public or private school of their choice, student achievement would rise dramatically.*

As you read, consider the following questions:

1. What did economist Caroline M. Hoxby call school choice?

2. According to the author, what happened to poorly performing traditional public schools in Michigan and Arizona when just 6 percent of their students left for charter schools?

3. How much would student achievement rise if students in kindergarten through twelfth grade were allowed to choose the private or public school of their choice, according to Murray?

For too long, families in California and across the country have assumed that poor-quality schools are an inner-city problem plaguing low-income parents who cannot afford to move near supposedly superior suburban schools. At more than one in 10 California public schools in neighborhoods with median home price approaching, and even exceeding, $1 million, less than half of students in at least one grade are below proficiency levels in English or math on state tests. Hundreds more affluent, suburban high schools statewide are graduating students who are not college-ready.

Given the current housing market, middle-income families may find themselves trapped in homes they can barely afford to keep and cannot afford to sell at a loss—all to be near "free" public schools that fail to deliver. Putting parents in charge of their children's education dollars would help.

Competition Works

Replacing the ossified monopoly system of assigned government schooling with a competitive, diversified education marketplace would introduce powerful incentives for all schools to perform. Money would follow students to any district-run or independent charter public school, regardless of family income or address. Universal vouchers, tuition tax-credit-scholarships, and education savings accounts (ESAs) would help parents in all income brackets send their children to private, nongovernment schools, which are about half as expensive as public schools, on average. Hundreds of scientific analyses spanning three decades also show competition works.

In their review of more than 200 scientific analyses of the effects of competition on traditional district public schools and students, researchers from Columbia University Teachers College conclude, "A sizable majority of these studies report beneficial effects of competition across all outcomes," including improved public school student performance, higher graduation rates, greater public-school efficiency, smaller class sizes, better teacher salaries, and improved housing values. Not one of the analyses found that competition harms the performance of public-school students.

Harvard University economist Caroline M. Hoxby finds that allowing parents to send their children to any public school regardless of where they live "is one of the most powerful market forces in American education," improving "productivity by simultaneously raising achievement and lowering spending." Competition from charter schools turbo-charges those results.

Even poorly performing traditional public schools in Michigan and Arizona raised annual math and reading scores once just six percent of their students began leaving for charter schools. The competitive effects of charter schools are so strong, in fact, that performance gaps between inner-city Phoenix public schools and surrounding suburban schools could be closed within a decade—without spending a penny more.

The Success of Charter Schools

Nationwide, charter schools educate a higher proportion of students from disadvantaged socioeconomic backgrounds.

Charter Schools Offer Increased Quality Through Competition

While competitive effects from charter schools are not as extensive as many advocates had hoped for, our research has uncovered some reasons why this may be so: resistance from officials who don't like charter schools; policies that shield districts and schools from feeling the financial consequences of failing to attract students; increasing enrollments because of demographic changes; a belief among traditional public school leaders that charters are not doing innovative things that are worthy of imitation. Our research also uncovered evidence that traditional public schools *are* reacting to charter school competition when they have reason to feel threatened. Principals report they change educational and administrative procedures when they feel competitive pressure, and districts adopt new programs when they can clearly see that parents want those programs. Those who believe traditional public schools can be driven to improve efficiency and achievement from competition can take heart from these findings.

Paul Teske, Mark Schneider, Jack Buckley, and Sara Clark,
"Does Charter School Competition Improve Traditional Public
Schools?," Manhattan Institute for Policy Research, June 2000.

Charter students are also more likely to be proficient on state math and reading exams, 3.2 and 5.2 percent respectively, even though charter schools in some states receive only 40 percent of traditional district public funding. The proficiency advantage is even greater in states where charter schools are well established. In California, for example, charter 4th graders are 10 percent more likely to be proficient in reading and math compared to their traditional public school peers.

Adding competition from private schools multiplies those effects. American higher education is the envy of the world in large part because education funding follows students to the schools of their choice, public or private. If K–12 education operated that way, research suggests the ensuing competition would raise student achievement 28 percent, again without spending a penny more.

School Choice Equals School Success

The empirical evidence shows that simply giving parents more freedom to choose their children's schools, public or private, yields the same gains in math achievement on the National Assessment of Educational Progress, often referred to as the Nation's Report Card, as raising per-pupil spending by more than $3,000 or increasing the median household income by $7,300, in current dollars. Low-income students who use vouchers to attend private schools also graduate at rates almost 60 percent higher than students in selective public high schools, and nearly 80 percent higher than students in regular public schools.

In none of the 13 states and the District of Columbia that have private school voucher and tuition tax-credit-scholarship programs has public school funding declined. In fact, it increased an average of five percent annually in real, inflation-adjusted terms.

An analysis by Johns Hopkins University statistician Susan Aud for the Milton and Rose D. Friedman Foundation [for Educational Choice] found those programs "have saved a total of nearly half a billion dollars." She adds, "School choice allows students to attend the schools of their choice at a lower cost than they would incur in the public school system, contrary to the dire fiscal speculations of its critics."

Freedom may not be free, but when it comes to education reform, it's a lot more effective, and less expensive, than the status quo.

"One of the major reasons charter schools have become such a hot topic recently is because there are numerous federal grants available for states that allow them."

Charter Schools Draw Money Away from Public Schools

Trent Moore

Trent Moore is a reporter for the Cullman Times, *a daily newspaper in Alabama. In the following viewpoint, he explores the opposition of many Alabama parents to legislation allowing charter schools in the state. Moore finds that many parents fear that charter schools will draw money from traditional public schools. Moore reports that many legislators, parents, and teachers also believe that the charter school model would not be a good fit in Alabama.*

As you read, consider the following questions:

1. As of 2010, how many states does Moore indicate have not passed charter school legislation?

2. According to Moore, how much money could Alabama receive in Race to the Top grants if it approves charter school legislation?

3. Why does Anita Nelson view charter schools as a slap in the face to teachers?

For Betty Marks, of Fairview [Alabama], there are a lot of ways to fix education in the state of Alabama—but charter schools aren't the answer.

"I don't like it at all and think it should stay out of our state," the local mother said. "I just don't think it's a suitable option for Alabama."

Chad Johnson, father of a Fairview student, agreed that he believes charter schools would hurt the local schools in Cullman County.

"Most of us grew up in this school system and I think we need to take care of it, first," he said. "We need to work with what we have, not open a bunch of new schools."

Charter Schools in Alabama?

Charter schools—which are currently being considered by the state legislature—operate as public institutions, but can be more flexible because they're not bound by as much red tape and regulations as traditional public schools. Charters must meet state academic standards, have the same number of annual school days and follow all civil rights laws against discrimination.

But, charter schools often operate without requirements that students live in certain neighborhoods and aren't held to the state's teacher tenure law. The main focus of charter schools is to improve low-performing schools, or to offer a more specialized focus.

Alabama is one of 11 states that has never passed charter school legislation, though Gov. Bob Riley and the state school board would like to see that changed.

But, many local education officials—as well as the politically influential Alabama Education Association—have opposed charters.

If a new law is passed, the decision to allow a charter school would likely be left up to each local school system, though there are some instances where the Alabama State Department of Education could make the decision. Existing traditional schools could also be converted into charters.

"Charter schools are there to fill a gap when traditional schools are failing," state education spokesman Michael Sibley told the Associated Press. "There's no expectation that we're going to see a ton of charter schools popping up all over the state."

Funding Tied to Innovation

One of the major reasons charter schools have become such a hot topic recently is because there are numerous federal grants available for states that allow them.

If legislation is approved, Alabama would receive 40 points in its 500-point federal application for Race to the Top grants [a competitive funding program run by the federal government], potentially worth $200 million.

"You'd have to get everything else almost perfect to have even a fighting chance," State Superintendent of Education Joe Morton said of the application's point structure. "If you have 40 states ahead of you at the start line, you've got to really run twice as fast to catch them. That's why it's important to address this issue now."

The grants are part of the American Recovery and Reinvestment Act, and will be given to states willing to try school innovation and reform, such as charter schools, according to the Department of Education.

Alabama's Educational Future

Alabama senate majority leader Zeb Little (D-Cullman) said he believes Alabama can reach the 500-point goal without passing a charter law.

"To accept the charter school money would require certain legislation to comply with federal regulations," he said. "I think we'll be able to get the federal money without resorting to charter schools. Ultimately, I believe we're going to be able to get those funds."

Morton said he believes charter schools are a move in the right direction for the future of education in Alabama.

"We do ourselves and, more important, our children a disservice when we do not use the abundance of our political and educational will to reach the lowest-performing schools in the state and possibly offer better alternatives," Morton said. "An independent charter school can provide better opportunities, increase accountability and foster educational excellence under the guiding principles and governance of a legislative charter, while traditional schools simultaneously benefit from their existence."

Local Thoughts on Charters

Superintendents of both local school systems in Cullman County—as well as many teachers and principals—have expressed concerns about charter legislation.

Cullman County Board of Education Superintendent Hank Allen said he is reluctant to embrace the idea.

"I'm personally not in favor of it," he said. "It's sort of like having a road or highway that you can't take care of, then adding a new highway that you're going to have to take care of. That's the analogy I would use, because I believe we should first take care of what we have, before talking about adding charter schools."

With funding at a critical low, Allen said he hopes the focus can remain on schools already in existence.

"It's not so much that charter schools are a bad idea, or something that's not probably good for the students, it's just the fact that we need to do a better job of funding the schools we already have, before we start surveying that," he said. "We're in dire straits and looking at a financial train wreck pretty soon, so why add another track that might not be successful?"

Judging the Ultimate Benefit

Cullman City Schools Superintendent Dr. Jan Harris said she does see some merit in charter schools, but does not believe they would benefit Alabama.

"Competition is always a good thing, however, I believe charter schools should come under the umbrella of the State Department of Education," she said. "They should have to adhere to the same federal and state regulations as public schools. My fear for charter schools is, if they don't have to adhere to these standards, you have an uneven playing field funded with the public's money."

Harris said she expects the charter debate to continue for some time.

"Education is a state function and I'm not in favor of education being a federal issue," she said. "Education is not mentioned in the constitution, therefore it is a state function. It should be led through local boards and by the character and people of the community."

Teacher Concerns

Neva Hite, a first-grade teacher at Fairview Elementary School, said she fears charter schools could rob public schools of needed funding.

The only positive, Hite said, would be additional freedom afforded to teachers at charter schools.

"I do think we're professional enough to teach by guidelines, or a course of study, because one specific program doesn't fit every child," she said. "I don't think we all fit in one little box, so that freedom could potentially be a benefit."

Reading teacher Anita Nelson, at Fairview Elementary School, said looser restrictions on teacher certification in charter schools could be a bad thing.

"Up to 25 percent of their teachers don't have to be certified by state standards," she said. "We have a lot of teachers working hard and that is a slap in the face to teachers who push themselves to be better."

Becky Eason, with the Cullman Area Career Center, said she is concerned about how career and technical classes would be handled if charter schools became prevalent in the state.

"I understand that Gov. Riley wants to model us after the charter laws in Florida," she said. "I actually called relatives out there, who told me everyone wants their son or daughter in a charter school. I'm inclined to think that it seems unfair that it would be a public school, alleviated from some of the rules we have.... How that could affect career and technical education is unknown."

Fairview Elementary School Principal Jessica Johnson said the issue is simple for her: If it hurts public school funding, she is opposed.

"The concept takes away money from local schools, so I'm not in favor of that because of funding," she said.

Local Legislators Are Opposed to Charters

The charter school law is facing an uphill battle in the state legislature, and members of the local delegation have all expressed concerns about the plan.

Rep. Jeremy Oden (R-Eva) said he sees the positives, but thinks we should first focus on the existing public schools in the state.

"Those are public education dollars pulled and put into another public setting," he said. "Why not pull those and put them in what we have now? Our schools are in a critical place and we need to take care of them."

By taking federal Race to the Top funds, Oden said Alabama would also be accepting additional federal stipulations.

"There is a lot of money out there, but what we don't realize is that if we go after that, we're bringing down federal regulations that come with that money," he said. "My constituents have said they don't want any new federal regulations, because that money has strings attached."

Rep. James Fields (D-Cullman) said he is still researching the proposed charter school legislation, though he is unsure if it will fit the needs of Alabama students.

"I haven't looked at the entire bill and I'm still trying to figure out if it will take money from our public school systems," he said. "But, right now, I would not be in favor of charter schools, because I would want to support our local schools."

Though charter schools work in other parts of the nation, Little said he does not believe the concept is feasible in rural Alabama.

"Our public school funding is already based on their enrollment, so we can't just drop that by pulling kids out and putting them into charter schools," he said. "The goal is to run a tighter ship, but the people I've talked to in education don't say that model will work here. I'm open to anything to make our schools better, but what I'm not open to is taking public money away from our public schools right now when they're hurting."

"The cash [for eleven charter schools in South Carolina] would come from local school districts that say they already are cash strapped, reeling from state budget cuts and prepping for even more."

Charter Schools Are Entitled to Local Educational Funds

Gina Smith

Gina Smith is a reporter for the State. *In the following viewpoint, she details the controversy over a South Carolina bill requiring local school districts to allocate local property tax dollars to charter schools. Under the old law, state-approved charter schools were funded by only federal and state dollars; under the new one, charters would receive local funds as well. Charter school operators argue that, as public schools, they are entitled to the funds, while public school district officials point out that they are suffering under budget cuts and that there is no money in the local budget to share with charter schools.*

As you read, consider the following questions:

1. According to the author, how much funding in local tax dollars annually will the South Carolina bill give to eleven charter schools in the state?

2. How much money does the author say that the charter school in Calhoun Falls would cost the local school district if the legislation passes?

3. Instead of allocating local tax funds, from where do school district officials believe the money to fund charter schools should come?

A charter school in Abbeville County [South Carolina] relies on volunteers to repair its plumbing and electrical systems. Spaghetti suppers help make the payroll.

A charter school in Spartanburg is staying open, thanks, in part, to contest money won from a department store.

Those two charter schools, and nine others around the state, say they are doing a good job of educating students but getting the short end of the financial stick. Without an infusion of cash, several say they will close.

House lawmakers are expected to debate this week [February 13–15, 2011] a controversial bill that would give the eleven charter schools nearly $21 million a year in local property tax dollars. That amount would increase if their enrollment increases.

The cash would come from local school districts that say they already are cash strapped, reeling from state budget cuts and prepping for even more. They say they cannot afford to share their local property tax dollars with the eleven charter schools.

The districts already have laid off teachers and staffers, eliminated programs and, in a couple of cases, are closing or have closed schools to save money.

In one case, for example, a local school district closed a school to save money. Community members then reopened the school as a charter school and, now, want local tax money to operate it.

Its students are public school students, too, its principal says, and their parents pay taxes.

The answer from public schools? "We're struggling too."

Spaghetti Suppers and Scrap Metal

In 2007, the Abbeville County school board was in a bind. Several mills had closed in the community, resulting in fewer students and less money for schools.

"We were the only district at that time that was so small and still had three high schools," said Ivan Randolph, superintendent of the Abbeville school district. "So I recommended we close the smallest one (Calhoun Falls) and save money."

Community members, not wanting their children bused to another school, reopened Calhoun Falls as a charter school.

Charter schools are public schools that anyone can open if they can win approval from their local school board or the state. A charter school must meet all of the state's academic standards, and students take the same standardized tests as given at traditional public schools. But the charters are freed of many state requirements to, hopefully, encourage new approaches to educating students.

Charters can be approved by local school districts, in which case they get local tax money, or the state.

The catch? Operated as a state-approved charter school, Calhoun Falls does not get local tax dollars from the Abbeville school district. It has to survive on federal and state dollars only.

Community members now collect and recycle soda cans and scrap metal to keep the lights on and pay the teachers at Calhoun Falls. Teachers earn $20,000 to $30,000 a year less than they would in traditional schools, but some still donate some of their pay each month to keep the school open.

Every other Sunday, the community gathers in the school cafeteria for a $6-a-plate supper of spaghetti, meatloaf or some other dish to keep the school running.

Struggling to Survive

"We survive day-to-day," said Calhoun Falls principal Deirdre McCullough, adding she doesn't mind sweeping the gym's floor. "We have a heart for these children. We know a lot of these children have financial challenges and other challenges in their lives, and we have a calling to be here, to give them the best chance they can."

In 2010, the school was rated as "below average" on its state report card. As a result, Calhoun Falls' 205 students are free to transfer to a nearby school that gets local money.

"But they want to stay here," said McCullough. "Their parents want them to stay here. We're very small, and we can meet the individual needs of a child in a way other schools can't."

If the proposal before the House becomes law, the Abbeville school district—which voted to close Calhoun Falls—would have to take the school back under its financial wing. But, this time, the school board would have no input into how it's run because it is now a charter school.

Calhoun Falls would cost the school district $370,000 a year. Superintendent Randolph has said the district would have to cut about nine teaching jobs at its other schools to support Calhoun Falls and other virtual charters that Abbeville students attend. The district already has cut its budget by about 20 percent in the past four years, eliminating some positions and furloughing teachers.

"When the charter school was opened, it was made clear what the money situation would be," Randolph said. "Now, it

The Charter School Funding Gap

School funding—and how the traditional mechanisms impede education reform—is fast becoming the next major area of focus for education policy makers. While the first 14 years of the charter movement focused on giving parents more innovative schools with higher academic standards than were found in the conventional system, those same years witnessed a growing awareness that funding laws and formulae in most states are severely flawed. Many policy makers and even advocates failed to realize those problems until the new charter laws had already been set in motion. Eleven state supreme courts have held that charter schools are public schools and that their students are entitled to the same public financial commitment as non-charter public school students. If charter school students are to be funded at the same level as other public school students, the causes of the funding gaps must be identified and corrected.

"Solving the Charter School Funding Gap,"
Center for Education Reform, 2005.

looks like we may get them again. If we have to fund the (Calhoun Falls), it will negatively impact our existing schools."

A Matter of Fairness

McCullough points out her students are public school students, and the school district is keeping the local tax dollars that their parents pay without having to educate their children.

"The law needs to be revised so that all public school students have the same rights to their parents' tax (money) even if they attend a charter school," McCullough said.

(While a 2006 law exempted owner-occupied homes from paying local property taxes for school operations, homeowners still pay for school construction bonds with those tax dollars.)

McCullough said she empathizes with struggling school districts. But she thinks there are places they could cut, including school administrators and athletic departments.

Local Districts in Trouble

S.C. superintendents and school board members say they hold no ill will against charter schools. The Abbeville school district, for example, donated the building that the Calhoun Falls charter uses.

But, they say, the financial pie isn't big enough to be cut up any more. Districts already are struggling with state budget cuts and the loss of federal stimulus money, and more state budget cuts are expected this year.

They say these state-approved charter schools agreed to forgo local money and should stick to the agreement.

"There's been so many cuts already," said Donnie Wilson, chief financial officer of the Kershaw County school district. "School districts can't afford it. This adds fuel to an already horribly burning fire."

However, under the House proposal, nearly every S.C. school district, including Kershaw, would have to take money from traditional schools and use it on the state-approved charters.

Instead of that, school districts want lawmakers to give charter schools more state money.

"If charter schools need more money and the state wants to give it to them, then they should go do it—with state dollars," said Kershaw County superintendent Frank Morgan, whose district would send $250,000 to charter schools if the bill passes. Already, the district has cut $12 million, or 17 percent of its budget, in the past two years.

Hanging in There

The eleven state-approved charter schools say some new funding solution needs to be found fast if they are to survive.

Those schools include popular virtual charter schools, where students take courses online, and high-performing brick-and-mortar charters.

For example, Spartanburg Charter School scored well on its 2010 report card and has a waiting list for several of its grades. But, because it gets no property tax money from the local school district, the school's future is unsure despite winning $500,000 in an online contest from the Kohl's department store chain.

"It's interesting how we can get great results on one-third of the money that the regular schools get," said John von Rohr, principal at Spartanburg Charter. "It's because our teachers make less. We're (also) not part of the state retirement system because we can't afford it."

Von Rohr dreams of replacing his school's original windows with new, energy-efficient ones. He says he is hopeful the state will find a way to make the finances work.

"We're barely surviving, and we're a public school that does everything any other public school does," von Rohr said. "This comes down to treating every public school child the same in this state."

Local school districts say they are in the same boat.

"Look around the state," Kershaw's Wilson said. "There are small (traditional, public schools) also closing because of money.

"We're struggling too."

Periodical and Internet Sources Bibliography

The following articles have been selected to supplement the diverse views presented in this chapter.

Ralph Bailey — "On Charter Schools, Educators Missing the Big Picture," Bakersfield.com, December 18, 2010. www.bakersfield.com.

Michel Faulkner — "Charter Schools a Path to American Dream," *Human Events*, October 12, 2010.

Sam Gill — "Charter Schools Are the Justin Bieber of Education Reform—A Fad Gone Too Far," *Christian Science Monitor*, February 18, 2011.

Benny L. Gooden — "Gooden Commentary: Schools Need Real Solutions," *Times Record* (Arkansas), October 3, 2010.

Mary Landrieu — "Opinion: The Important Role of Charter Schools," *The Hill* (blog), May 17, 2011. http://thehill.com.

Joyce McRath and Stanton Lawrence — "Charters Must Prove Their Effectiveness," St. Louis Today, April 12, 2011. www.stltoday.com.

Alexander Ooms — "The Performance of Denver's Charter Schools," *Education News Colorado* (blog), December 14, 2010. http://blog.ednews colorado.org.

Clarence Page — "Failing Charter Schools Hurt Reputation of Successes," *Houston Chronicle*, July 1, 2010.

Jason Richwine — "Charter Schools: A Welcome Choice for Parents," Heritage Foundation, August 30, 2010. www.heritage.org.

CHAPTER 2

Are Religious Charter Schools a Viable Choice?

Chapter Preface

Since America's founding, policy makers and citizens have recognized the need for a secular educational system that is free from religious conflict and influence—a system where children of different backgrounds could come together to learn secular American values and have access to a high-quality education. Such schools aided in the assimilation of immigrants, who were asked to learn American culture and the English language, as well as American history and civics. By the mid-nineteenth century, the United States had largely replaced parochial schools with secular ones, funded by public money.

Many Catholic immigrants, however, perceived a Protestant influence in American mainstream education and began to set up a competitive system of schools that would reflect their own Catholic values. These Catholic schools were run by religious clergy and were located mainly in large urban areas. Before long, secular education advocates as well as Protestant lawmakers began to champion legislation to prohibit public funding of any religious school. In 1875 President Ulysses S. Grant took up the cause, calling for a constitutional amendment that would mandate free public schools and outlaw the use of public money for religious schools. Under this amendment, religious schools would essentially become private schools, and parents—not taxpayers—would have to pay for the tuition. In a speech to a veterans' group in Des Moines, Iowa, in 1876, Grant maintained that it was essential to American education to keep church and state "forever separate" and called for a "good common-school education, unmixed with sectarian, pagan, or atheistical dogma."

Republican congressman James G. Blaine was the legislator who proposed Grant's amendment to the US Constitution. Known as the Blaine Amendment, it read that "no state shall make any law respecting an establishment of religion, or prohibiting the free exercise thereof; and no money raised by taxation in any State for the support of public schools, or derived from any public fund therefor, nor any public lands devoted thereto, shall ever be under the control of any religious sect; nor shall any money so raised or lands so devoted be divided between religious sects or denominations." The Blaine Amendment failed to pass and never became federal law.

Supporters of the Blaine Amendment turned to the states, where it was included in state constitutions drafted by new states accepted into the Union. Other states passed laws banning the use of public funds to support private religious schools; these laws are also called Blaine Amendments. These laws helped form the precedent of separation between church and state in American education, a tradition that sets out the principle that public school education should be free of religious influence and that religious schools should receive no public money.

This debate over public funding of religious education has been renewed by the emergence of religious charter schools. The following chapter examines the constitutionality, role, and value of religious charters, as well as whether financially challenged Catholic schools should be allowed to convert into charter schools.

"In an era of widespread public school failure and unprecedented diversity, religious charter schools have the potential to foster increased investment in the public school system among members of religious groups."

Religious Charters Are Constitutional in Most Circumstances

Benjamin Siracusa Hillman

Benjamin Siracusa Hillman is a lawyer and commentator. In the following viewpoint, he argues that concerns about the constitutionality of religious public schools are overblown. Hillman contends that religious charters can take measures to ensure that they do not cross the constitutional line into promoting religion by requiring safeguards, such as a curriculum committee or an independent watchdog group to scrutinize classes and practices. This would protect the rights of students and guarantee that religious charters do not violate the constitutional separation of church and state.

As you read, consider the following questions:

1. What does Hillman predict will happen to religious minorities if society does not allow religious charter schools?

2. How does Hillman propose religious charter schools handle the ability to teach values that are different from the values of the larger community?

3. What kinds of school districts does Hillman argue are best equipped to create religious charter schools without discriminating against students who are not members of that religion?

Critics question why public schools should accommodate different religions. Some say public schools should teach shared American values and promote the assimilation of immigrants and religious minorities into American life; religious charter schools seem to work against this goal. Yet in creating school choice, urban districts have already abandoned the historical presumption that traditional public schools can serve everyone. Failing to accommodate religious minorities forces them to choose between participating in public education and maintaining their religion. When faced with this choice, many will abandon public education for home, virtual, or private schooling. Localities should consider these trends in deciding whether to accommodate religious minorities.

Self-Regulation Is Key

Religious charter schools also face accusations that their efforts to teach values and culture and accommodate religious observance cross the constitutional line into promoting religion. Critics claim that religious charter schools cannot maintain this line, and districts cannot police it, because the distinctions are unclear or cover up covert promotion of religious practice. Initially, districts can address this concern by scrutinizing proposed religious charter schools to ensure that they can comply with the First Amendment. They may wish to require safeguards, such as a curriculum committee that includes non-adherents who can vet the school's curriculum and practices. Once in operation, districts can, consistent with the Constitution, conduct regular on- and off-site reviews of a charter school's operations and materials. Religious charter schools also have a strong incentive to self-police, because they want to retain their funding. If they push the line, as TIZ [Tarek ibn Ziyad Academy, an academically successful religious charter school in Inver Grove Heights, Minnesota, with a primarily Muslim enrollment] has, they risk community criticism, court challenges, and potentially revocation. Books like Lawrence [D.] Weinberg's guide [*Religious Charter Schools: Legalities and Practicalities*], which applies First Amendment jurisprudence to hypothetical religious charter schools, make compliance easier.

Critics also fear that religious charter schools will discriminate against prospective attendees and employees, selecting them on the basis of religion. But charter schools must comply with Title VII [a federal law that prohibits discrimination by employers on the basis of race, color, religion, sex, and national origin] in hiring teachers. Like other employers whose jobs have disproportionate appeal to members of a particular group, religious charter schools must search broadly for employees to avoid disparate impact discrimination. They appear to do so; both Ben Gamla Charter School [a Jewish charter school in Hollywood, Florida] and Tarek ibn Ziyad Academy have teachers from varied religious backgrounds.

Welcoming Diversity

Charter schools, under most states' laws or if they receive federal funds, are required to admit students by lottery. This requirement should preempt potential discrimination and ensure that publicly funded schools remain open to attendees from all backgrounds. Self-segregation could lead to religious charter schools only serving their affiliated religions. Still, the example of Ben Gamla—where a significant minority of non-Jewish students has enrolled—demonstrates that parents may enroll their children in a religious charter school affiliated with a different religion. Religious private schools, especially Catholic schools, have long enrolled non-adherents whose parents felt that the schools offered a superior education, so it seems unwarranted to assume that religious charter schools will become de facto segregated.

Thorny Question

Finally, the difficult question arises of the extent to which religious charter schools should be able to teach values explicitly at odds with majority values. For example, should a religious charter school be able to teach that homosexuality is wrong, where other public schools in the district teach tolerance? To maintain neutrality, districts should allow religious charter schools the same latitude given other choice-based schools, which could conceivably be greater than what they allow traditional public schools. The autonomy of charter schools makes them unique within the public school system; if religious charter schools lose the ability to embrace their community's values, a key virtue will be lost.

The government cannot restrict the First Amendment rights of grant recipients as a condition of funding, provided that the protected conduct occurs "outside the scope of the federally funded program." But the government can constitutionally prohibit a grantee from using public funds toward specific purposes, and in the process decline to subsidize the exercise of a constitutional right. Applying this doctrine to the aforementioned example, in which a legislature has formalized nondiscrimination against gays and lesbians as public policy, the state may require that religious charter schools *not* teach disapproval of homosexuality during the school day. Less clear is whether the state could require that a religious charter school teach tolerance as a condition of participation in a charter school program, where such teachings would contradict the school's values. A court's analysis will depend on whether it perceives the teaching as the government's use of private speakers to transmit the government's educational message ("government speech"), or instead as the expenditure of public funds to facilitate the message of private speakers ("private speech"). If it views the message as private speech, it may strike down restrictions as viewpoint discrimination in violation of the First Amendment. On the other hand, if it views a charter school program as government speech transmitted through the medium of private speakers, or it views the message itself, even if private speech, as contrary to the very purposes for which the government funds charter schools, then it might uphold restrictions against a First Amendment challenge.

Judging Religious Charter

The hybrid public-private nature of charter schools makes it difficult to anticipate how a court would decide. Because the private operator typically chooses the curriculum, courts will most likely consider a charter school's speech as private speech funded by the government. As such, courts will likely prevent states from requiring that charter schools present a particular state-sanctioned viewpoint on controversial issues. Yet because charter schools operate as part of the public school system, courts will most likely uphold states' power to ensure that charters operate within the outer bounds of state public policy. Thus, on controversial subjects, religious charter schools could say something that does not conflict with state public policy or refrain from speaking entirely. This approach would be consistent with current practice, as many states already permit public schools and districts to take diverse approaches to controversial social or curricular issues like same-sex relationships or sex education.

The Ben Gamla Charter School

In late August 2007, the Ben Gamla Charter School opened its doors to approximately 400 students in Hollywood, Florida. Funded by public dollars and named for a first-century Jewish high priest who sought to introduce universal education, the school aimed to provide "a first-class academic program" featuring "a unique bilingual, bi-literate, and bi-cultural curriculum, which prepares students to have an edge in global competition through the study of Hebrew as a second language." Ben Gamla's director, Rabbi Adam Siegel, was unequivocal in explaining that the school was by no means religious. Despite some raised eyebrows and a brief suspension of Hebrew classes by the Broward County school district, the charter school appears to be thriving, and its founder plans to open additional Hebrew-language charter schools in the coming years.

The media attention it garnered notwithstanding, the Ben Gamla experiment is far from unique. Since the advent of the charter school movement in the early 1990s, a number of start-up schools have adopted similar, culture-oriented models. These controversial schools straddle long-standing disputes over religion, pedagogy, and the public fisc that date to the earliest incarnations of the public school system. From bitter conflict over the anti-Catholic character of the first common schools to modern controversies over school prayer and vouchers, public education has historically been a flashpoint of the hoary church-state debate.

"Church, Choice, and Charters: A New Wrinkle for Public Education?," Harvard Law Review, *April 2009.*

Finding Appropriate Spaces for Religious Charter Schools

Each school district will want to choose independently whether to have religious charter schools. Generally, religious charter schools will be most appropriate in large districts with significant numbers of religious minorities; in these districts, religious charter schools will help the state maximize the availability of satisfactory options while minimizing the chances of oppressing non-adherents. Smaller districts that cannot afford to support a variety of school choice options, or that do not have a diverse array of religious groups willing to create charter schools, may find direct accommodation of religious observance more feasible.

The *Zelman* Court [referring to *Zelman v. Simmons-Harris*, a 2002 Supreme Court case in which it was decided that school voucher plans were constitutional if they met certain criteria] cited neutrality among religions and a broad availability of religious and nonreligious choices as prominent factors in approving a voucher program. Districts that can support only a few religious charter schools should exercise caution before creating any. They otherwise risk favoring particular religious groups, which might exacerbate the paucity of schools conducive to the needs of religious minorities. Having only religious charter schools would also impinge on the conscience of students whose beliefs—religious or otherwise—conflict with those of religious charter schools in the district, and would violate *Zelman's* requirement that publicly funded schooling include viable nonreligious options. Larger districts that can support many types of schools are best equipped to create religious charter schools and still avoid discriminating against those who are not members of participating religious groups.

Similarly, religious charter schools are most appropriate in larger districts with a diverse array of religious groups willing to participate. Ensuring state neutrality among religious groups, as the Establishment Clause [of the First Amendment of the Constitution] demands, requires chartering agencies to evaluate prospective religious and nonreligious charter schools using identical, religiously neutral standards. Ongoing evaluation also must take place. Larger districts are capable of uniformly applying neutral standards to a diversity of religious groups, enabling them to avoid the entanglement concerns that arise when the government works with only a few religious groups.

More Advantages of Larger Districts

Larger, heterogeneous districts may also be able to accommodate more efficiently the needs of their religious minority communities in religious charter schools. Constitutionally, traditional public schools can choose to accommodate attendees' needs. Parents cannot force public schools to furnish accommodations, however, and schools' willingness to accommodate varies. When public schools are unwilling to accommodate, or if religious groups' values are too diverse to adequately serve everyone in one school, religious charter schools can help. Smaller districts tend to be more homogeneous and in such districts, it may be easier and more cost-effective to accommodate the values and observance of a few religious minority attendees within a traditional public school.

Finally, only large districts with a diverse system of school choice at the district level can ameliorate the fear that schools with religiously defined normative frameworks will oppress non-adherents. Because all charter schools are based upon choice and the option of exit, charter schools arguably have a greater warrant than traditional public schools to maintain a particular normative mission. As discussed earlier, the availability of choice creates a situation in which "like-minded teachers and students can affirmatively choose to invest themselves in one school instead of another based on distinct normative claims embodied" in each school's mission. Additionally, in a choice-based system, schools must openly publicize their values so that families can make informed choices; as *Vanguard* [*Daugherty v. Vanguard* is a 2000 US District Court decision that held that Vanguard Charter Academy in Wyoming, Michigan, did not violate a student's constitutional right by teaching morals based on Christianity] illustrates, having dissatisfied parents breeds litigation. Such a system of choice, featuring schools with open and competing normative missions, only works if there is a varied selection of schools from which to choose. Offering this type of selection is not feasible in most smaller districts.

The Benefits of Religious Charters

Like other charter schools, religious charter schools consciously ground themselves in the values and culture of a particular community. For students and families who find the values underlying public school education to be alienating, they can offer a more appealing environment. For religiously observant students, religious charter schools provide the opportunity to maintain one's religion without sacrificing the benefits of a general education and a diverse environment. More broadly, they give religious minority groups the opportunity to design charter schools that reflect their values. Families benefit from the energy that religious groups bring to education. In today's pluralistic society, religious charter schools promote democracy by empowering members of religious minority groups to participate in the public sphere.

In an era of widespread public school failure and unprecedented diversity, religious charter schools have the potential to foster increased investment in the public school system among members of religious groups. Ultimately, by empowering religious groups to bring their values and culture into a public school system that may otherwise ignore them, religious charter schools further the ability of urban public schools to meet their students' needs.

| *"Charter schools with special religious and cultural missions may be staying just this side of the law, but their missions run counter to the entire history of American public education."*

Religious Charters Are Unconstitutional

Susan Jacoby

Susan Jacoby is an author, a reporter, and program director of the Center for Inquiry. In the following viewpoint, Jacoby states that it violates the First Amendment to have charter school promoters with specific religious and cultural agendas create schools that reflect religious beliefs and contradict accepted science. Jacoby insists that if parents want their children to have a religious education, they should pay for it themselves and not use public tax dollars for the privilege. Religious education does not belong in public settings, Jacob maintains, regardless of whether parents approve of it.

As you read, consider the following questions:

1. According to Jacoby, how many American children attend charter schools?

Susan Jacoby, "Many Charter Schools Continue to Defy Church-State Separation," copyright © 2010 by Susan Jacoby. Originally appeared in *The Washington Post* (December 1, 2010). Reprinted by permission of Georges Borchardt Inc., on behalf of the author.

2. What percentage of charter schools in Texas does the *Dallas Morning News* report have close ties to religious institutions?

3. What does Jacoby indicate as a continuing problem in charter schools with strong ties to religion?

More than 1.5 million American children now attend charter schools, thanks to a movement asserting that whatever is wrong with American public education can be fixed by what amounts to semiprivate—publicly funded but privately managed—school enclave within the larger system. Many representatives of both the cultural right and left have signed on to this Charter of Wishful Thinking, which continues to be seen as a panacea for the ills of public schools even though the most comprehensive evaluation of charter schools, by Stanford University's Center for [Research on] Education Outcomes, reveals "in unmistakable terms that, in the aggregate, charter students are not faring as well" in terms of academic performance as students in comparable public schools. Even worse, and equally unmistakable, is the fact that charter school promoters with specific religious and cultural agendas around the country are using every possible means to skirt the First Amendment and obtain public support for private aims.

A Serious Problem Is Being Ignored

I have written about this subject many times, as the number of charter schools with close ties to religion continues to increase. Hardly anyone of any political persuasion seems to care—with the notable exception of a few watchdog groups such as the Secular Coalition for America and Americans United for Separation of Church and State.

The *Dallas Morning News* reports that more than 20 percent of charter schools in Texas have close links to religious institutions. For instance, the Advantage Academy in Duncan-

Religion and Education

Allen Beck, the [Advantage Academy's] founder and a former Assemblies of God pastor, hopes to instill morals and ethics in students as they learn to count and read. "America is in a battle between secularity and biblical thinking," he said. "I want to fuse the two together in a legal way."

Jessica Meyers,
"Charter Schools with Ties to Religious Groups
Raise Fears About State Funds' Use,"
Dallas Morning News, *November 22, 2010.*

ville, TX, was founded by a former pastor in the Assemblies of God. School officials openly announce that their curriculum teaches creationism and intelligent design and no one in charge of public education in Texas seems to know—or care— that the teaching of creationism has been banned by the U.S. Supreme Court.

Charter schools in Texas receive tax funds for teacher salaries and textbooks and religious groups can apply for state approval if they establish a separate nonprofit foundation to administer public funds. Talk about a distinction without a difference. If schools founded and run by ministers, teaching classes that reflect religious belief and contradict accepted science, do not violate the First Amendment, what does?

The Dangers of Religious Education in Public Schools

A majority of religiously affiliated charter schools are run by right-wing evangelical Christians, but Catholics, Jews and Muslims are also getting a piece of the action. In Houston, the Harmony charter schools are controlled by Turkish Muslims spreading the philosophy of one imam. In many states, Roman Catholic parochial schools are being turned into publicly supported charter schools with the proviso that they abandon the teaching of religion and provide purely secular instruction. Since, in many instances, the faculty remains the same, does anyone think that these religious schools are going to magically morph into secular schools? If these parochial schools were so wonderful in the first place, why haven't they been supported by the church and tuition-paying parents?

Schools emphasizing Hebrew language and culture are different, because they do not have overt ties to Jewish religious institutions. But they are no less questionable than the charter schools inspired by evangelical Christians, Muslims or Catholic bishops looking for a way out of their financial dilemma. In June, the *New York Times* published a glowing article about the Hebrew Language Academy [HLA] Charter School in Brooklyn—an institution that isn't run by a rabbi or synagogue but nevertheless, in my view, represents much that is wrongheaded about the charter school movement. Each class has both a Hebrew and English teacher. Children receive an hour of formal Hebrew instruction a day and Israeli history is stressed. The students watch Israeli children's TV and celebrate Israeli Independence Day in addition to American holidays.

About two-thirds of the students at HLA are white and another third are African American or Latino, selected, as required by law, from a lottery of applicants. The school is forbidden to inquire about faith but many of the white students are Jewish and several parents told the *Times* that were it not for the free public charter school, they would have sent their children to Jewish day schools that cost $20,000 a year. Michael Steinhardt, a retired hedge fund manager, is the "angel" who adds his own donations—several hundred thousands of dollars a year—to HLA's public funds. The principal is Steinhardt's daughter, Sara Berman, who asserts, "To say that you can't learn about what it is like to go to a shuk in Jerusalem because it's too complicated or tied to religion and politics, that's just not the case." Hebrew has nothing to do with Judaism? That would certainly surprise a great many Talmudic [authoritative body of Jewish tradition] scholars.

Using Tax Dollars for Religious Instruction

If parents want their children to learn Hebrew, Greek, Chinese, Arabic or Spanish in elementary school, they should do it the old-fashioned way—pay for it themselves. It is simply appalling that tax dollars are being used to fund a school that some Jewish parents consider an excellent alternative to a private religious school. It is just as appalling to spend public funds on providing an education that Muslim or evangelical Christian parents find more agreeable than the education in public schools. Language courses, and classes that emphasize other cultures, certainly have a place in public schools—but only as electives. Charter schools with special religious and cultural missions may be staying just this side of the law, but their missions run counter to the entire history of American public education, which is supposed to promote assimilation along with fundamental learning.

There is, of course, an urgent need to improve public education. If I were a parent in an urban neighborhood with poor public schools, I'd jump at the chance to have my children attend a school whose funds are supplemented by a private donation of several hundred thousand dollars—whether the children are required to study Hebrew, Arabic or Swahili. But donations from individuals with their own agendas cannot and are not intended to improve public education for everyone. The best article on this subject is Diane Ravitch's recent essay, in the *New York Review of Books* about the movie *Waiting for "Superman."*

Dr. Ravitch, who served in the U.S. Department of Education under Presidents George H.W. Bush and Bill Clinton, is the nation's most distinguished historian of education and was an early supporter of charter schools. She has changed her mind as a result of the disappointing performance results and the cultural divisiveness promoted by charters at public expense.

Corruption Is Rife in Religious Charters

A continuing problem—one most evident in schools with strong ties to religions—is the use of charter school funds by unscrupulous founders to provide jobs for relatives and church members. In Texas, which continues to authorize new religious-connected charters, there have been numerous scandals of this nature. In Houston, the Rev. Harold Wilcox was indicted six years ago for embezzling both state and federal funds at a school that held classes in a Baptist church sanctuary. Wilcox paid himself $210,000 annually to run the school. Ten years ago, the state investigated Dallas's Rylie Family Faith Academy and found dozens of family and church members on the payroll. The school supposedly cleaned up its act, and Rylie Family Faith still operates two charter schools. One can only imagine the bellows of rage from the religious right, which considers teachers' unions a stand-in for Satan, if similar nepotism was discovered in a public school

It is truly deplorable that both conservative and liberal politicians, from the White House to the state houses, continue to hop aboard the charter school bandwagon without regard for the daily assaults on the separation of church and state—and the concept of civic unity—that these schools represent. Forget about *E pluribus unum*. That's so eighteenth century.

"*Across the country, church leaders can and do run [charter] schools, but most are run through separate nonprofits or management organizations, not the churches directly.*"

Religious Charters Can Provide a Secular Education

Grace Rauh

Grace Rauh is a political reporter for the New York Sun *and* NY1 *news channel. In the following viewpoint, she chronicles the effort of a Harlem, New York, church to overturn a state law that bars religious organizations from managing charter schools, even if the schools do not teach religion. Rauh reports that the head of the New Horizon Church of New York, Michel Faulkner, argues that religious institutions are perfectly able to uphold the values of the separation of church and state and should be allowed to create independent, successful charter schools in accordance with existing laws.*

Grace Rauh, "Church Sues for Right to Run Charter," *New York Sun*, October 1, 2007. All rights reserved. Reproduced by permission.

As you read, consider the following questions:

1. What is the significance of the Khalil Gibran International Academy to Reverend Michel Faulkner, as reported by Rauh?

2. What is the New York State Charter Schools Act of 1998, as described by Rauh?

3. According to Rauh, why has the Ben Gamla Charter School been controversial?

A Harlem church is suing the state [of New York] in an attempt to overturn a law that bars religious organizations from running charter schools even if the schools don't teach religion, a move likely to prompt new debate about the separation between church and state.

The Reverend Michel Faulkner of New Horizon Church [of New York] said he wants to open a charter school in Harlem or Washington Heights that would be affiliated with his church, but would not have a religious component to the curriculum. If successful, Rev. Faulkner could change the face of new charter schools, allowing churches, synagogues, and mosques to operate them in New York.

Changing the Law

Across the country, church leaders can and do run such schools, but most are run through separate nonprofits or management organizations, not the churches directly.

Rev. Faulkner could apply to open a charter school through a nonprofit organization separate from his church, but he said yesterday he's not interested in that approach.

"I just feel like it's not fair," he said. "We, as a religious institution, can certainly uphold the values of separation between church and state."

He said he was galvanized to file the suit after seeing an Arabic-language school, the Khalil Gibran International Academy, open in Brooklyn this fall [in 2007]. The public school was founded by a devout Muslim, but is not affiliated with Islam or any religious institution. Rev. Faulkner said he saw a connection between his would-be charter school and Khalil Gibran.

"If an Arabic school can start up, certainly New Horizon can start a charter school in order to promote great quality education," he said.

Doubts About the Law and the School

A spokesman for Americans United for Separation of Church and State, Joseph Conn, said the suit sounded groundless.

"It seems unlikely to me that a church would want to run a school that is devoid of religious content," he said. "The whole purpose of the church is to teach and spread religion."

The executive director of Gotham Legal Foundation, Jay Golub, said Rev. Faulkner is a community leader and the best person in his neighborhood to run a charter school. Mr. Golub, who ran for public advocate in 2005, said his foundation filed the suit on behalf of the church in federal court this week. He called it a case of "pure religious discrimination."

"The New York [State] Charter Schools Act is nothing more than an attempt by the State to erect a barrier for those who express their religious beliefs from access to public resources," the suit states.

The Existing Law Is Challenged

The suit is challenging a portion of the New York [State] Charter Schools Act of 1998, which says a charter will not be issued to a school that is run by a religious organization or a school where religious doctrine is taught. It is asking the federal court to deem unconstitutional a portion of the state constitution that bars public dollars for education purposes from going to religious institutions.

The arguments of the suit link it to the debate surrounding school vouchers—publicly funded scholarships to private schools used in a growing number of states and cities. Many students use the vouchers to attend parochial schools. Critics of vouchers often endorse charter schools as a better alternative because they avoid sending public funds to religious institutions.

Charter schools with strong religious ties are often challenged. A charter school in Florida with a Hebrew theme, the Ben Gamla Charter School, has faced criticism from its local school board for using textbooks with some religious themes.

A charter school group run by an evangelical Christian minister, the National Heritage Academies, was the target of a lawsuit by the Michigan chapter of the ACLU [American Civil Liberties Union]. The group claimed that a charter school run by National Heritage, the Vanguard School, was holding prayer sessions in schools.

The Key to the Issue

A senior fellow at the education policy think tank Education Sector, Steven Wilson, said the arrangements can be fine.

"The key is whether or not they are proselytizing," he said. "I don't see the reason why church leaders shouldn't be permitted—so long as it's open to all students regardless of faith, and so long as there's no religious teaching."

The chairman of the country's largest charter school, Donald Hense, said the constitutional separation between church and state should keep religious leaders far away from charter schools.

"Religious groups are interested first about whatever philosophy they proselytize," he said. "Public money should not be used to support that." He said he does not let religious leaders play any role at all in his school, the Friendship Public Charter School in Washington, D.C.

The CEO of the New York City [Charter School] Center, James Merriman, said he hasn't seen many examples in which churches have come forward and said they are disappointed they couldn't start a charter school.

He said he has seen instances in New York where members of a church parish have successfully sought a charter and opened a school outside of their church.

"It was their dream to have a school. A school that served not just the parishioners' children, but that served anyone within the community," he said.

| "*Although free from some regulations that apply to traditional public schools, charters are still public schools. That means they must be nonsectarian— neither promoting nor denigrating religion.*"

Religious Charters Do Not Serve the Common Good

Charles C. Haynes

Charles C. Haynes is an author, director of the Religious Freedom Education Project at the Newseum, and a senior scholar at the First Amendment Center. In the following viewpoint, he characterizes the recent trend of religious groups founding charter schools problematic. Haynes questions whether religious charter schools—even if they focus on providing a secular education—serve the common good and not just the interests of one religious group. He also maintains that it may not be in the interest of religious groups to create a faith-based school without a religious curriculum.

As you read, consider the following questions:

1. In 2008, how many schools does Haynes say were converted from Roman Catholic schools to charter schools in Washington, D.C.?

2. What phrase does Haynes identify as a "First Amendment oxymoron" and why?

3. According to the author, what is the basis of the controversy over the Ben Gamla Charter School?

On June 16 [2008], seven Roman Catholic schools in Washington, D.C., were transformed into seven public charter schools by a unanimous vote of the D.C. Public Charter School Board. It's a conversion of sorts—only in reverse.

The Charter School Bandwagon

Other religious communities around the nation are already on the charter bandwagon, opening Arabic charters without Islam and Hebrew charters without Judaism. Not to be left behind, a Protestant minister in Harlem is pressing to start what he claims will be a religion-free charter in his church building.

Strange as it may sound, this is a hot new trend in education: creating faith-based schools without the faith.

Establishing a charter requires shedding overt religious identity because "religious charter school" is a First Amendment oxymoron. Although free from some regulations that apply to traditional public schools, charters are still public schools. That means they must be nonsectarian—neither promoting nor denigrating religion.

The Bottom Line

So why do people of faith leap to schools of no faith? In the case of the Washington Catholic schools, it's all about the bottom line. As Archbishop Donald W. Wuerl told the *Washington Post*, "We simply don't have the resources to keep all those schools open."

With voucher proposals stalled in many state legislatures—or running up against state constitutional barriers—some Catholic dioceses and other religious groups are eyeing charter schools as a funding alternative.

But take the Catholic out of Catholic schools and what's left? According to the archbishop, "They will have the same teachers, the same kids, the same environment. There will still be a level of value formation."

What that will look like remains to be seen. At this point, it's hard to see how the schools can sustain the "same environment" given that charters must be nonsectarian in hiring, admission and curriculum.

The Challenge

But at least these Catholic schools are populated mostly by non-Catholic students. When charter schools are designed to attract students of one religion, being faith-based without the faith is a much greater challenge.

Consider last year's [2007's] controversy surrounding the opening of Ben Gamla Charter School in Florida, the nation's first Hebrew charter school. It took several tries before the school board approved the Hebrew curriculum because of concerns about religious bias in the materials.

Ben Gamla's start-up problems, however, haven't dissuaded Jewish community leaders in other states from undertaking similar efforts. An application was filed this month [June 2008] to open a Hebrew-language charter school in New York City.

Excluding faith from Hebrew charter schools doesn't seem to bother proponents. Philanthropist Michael Steinhardt, a backer of the New York school, was quoted last fall in the *New Jersey Jewish News* as envisioning "a nationwide system of Jewish charter schools focusing on Jewish elements, not on religious studies—which appeals only to a minority of Jews anyway—but on elements of Jewish culture that make us strong."

The Effects of Charter School Conversion on Religious Faith

Whether faiths will grow stronger with or apart from public money is certain to vary with many factors. Certainly, public funding is not a panacea but is a long-awaited opportunity to level the ideological playing field of education that has been sharply sloped in favor of the growth of superficial faith and secularism. . . . Surely, many religious schools may lose their spiritual "flavor" under public funding, but many are doing so currently apart from public money.

Whichever route religious schools decide upon, to keep faith strong, they should continue to provide costly educations, and they should never become complacent with the status quo.

Craig Engelhardt,
"The Religious School's Dilemma:
Take the Tax Money or Run?,"
Private School Monitor, *Spring 2009.*

Drawing the Line

What is complicated line-drawing for Jews is even more complex for Muslims. The current uproar over Tarek ibn Ziyad Academy [TIZA] in Minnesota underscores the pitfalls and challenges of attempting to separate Arabic culture and Islamic faith.

After news reports of possible mosque-state violations, the Minnesota Department of Education found TIZA generally in compliance with state law, ordering a few modest changes in school practice. But it won't be easy for school officials to remain neutral toward religion as required by the First Amendment in a school serving mostly Muslims who want and expect an environment that reflects Islamic values.

A Disturbing Trend

Even if all of these schools manage to satisfy the letter of the First Amendment (a big if), the trend toward faith-based schools without the faith is problematic for at least two reasons.

First, public schools were founded to educate youngsters of all races and creeds. Of course, parents have the right to send their children to religious or other private schools. Public schools, however, receive public support because they serve the common good—not just the interests of one group.

It's important to ask whether Hebrew and Arabic charter schools—filled with mostly Jewish and Muslim students, respectively—undermine the purpose of public schools by creating a balkanized system of public education.

Second, a faith-based school without the faith does religion no favors. Devout Christians, Jews, Muslims and others may be tempted to take the money and start the school. But substituting "culture" for "religion" is no way to advance the mission of faith.

Religious leaders beware. This Faustian bargain [a bargain made for present gain without regard for the future] isn't worth the spiritual cost.

> "Many Catholic education leaders say they can't compete with 'free' charter schools, even when recruiting Catholic families. Here's the solution: Make Catholic schools free, too."

Failing Catholic Schools Should Become Charter Schools

Chester E. Finn Jr. and Michael Petrilli

Chester E. Finn Jr. is an author, senior fellow at the Hoover Institution, senior editor of Education Next, *and president of the Thomas B. Fordham Institute. Michael Petrilli is a research fellow at the Hoover Institution and vice president for national programs and policy at the Thomas B. Fordham Institute. In the following viewpoint, they explore the option of financially failing Catholic schools in a number of American cities. Finn and Petrilli suggest that in situations where suburban Catholic communities cannot subsidize keeping urban Catholic schools open, they should consider allowing them to become religious charter schools. In that way, the government would be providing funding while still providing a quality education to students who need it.*

As you read, consider the following questions:

1. According to the Glover Park Group survey referred to by the authors, what percentage of Catholics view Catholic schools favorably?

2. How many Catholics in ten view "working with economically disadvantaged students" as the domain of public schools, according to the Glover Park Group survey?

3. What group of people do the authors determine can "generously support networks of Catholic schools that operate independently of Diocesan structures"?

The most impressive action that our team [researchers from a variety publications] spotted in urban Catholic education is around educating Catholic children. This shouldn't come as a huge surprise. The Church's primary mission, after all, is religious, not educational. That it should recommit itself to the spiritual development of its youngest members seems commonsensical. (Though as an unobservant Jew and a lapsed Catholic, perhaps our opinions on this matter don't count for much.)

The Case of Wichita

Wichita is the best example. Here the archdiocese promulgated a simple principle: Catholic schooling would be free to all parishioners. To make the financials work, the bishop asked all Church members to tithe a significant portion of their salaries, which largely went into the school operations fund. Parishioners responded enthusiastically. Today, all Wichita Catholics can send their children to parochial school. Tuition is no barrier. This is particularly important for the archdiocese's poor, urban families (yes, Wichita has some) who can benefit from the Church's religious and academic teachings. The Wichita example is striking for several reasons. First, it flies in the face of the conventional wisdom that Catholic school tuition must inevitably rise every year. It's true that costs are increasing. Without nuns or brothers to staff the schools, Catholic education systems must hire lay teachers and administrators and pay them competitive wages. But these costs don't have to be passed on to parents in the form of tuition; they can be subsidized by the Church as a whole.

Supporting Catholic Schools

If Wichita can do this, why can't other communities? Our survey shows that Catholics love their Catholic schools—88 percent view them favorably (versus 70 percent who hold that opinion of the pope). Sure, there are plenty of dioceses where practically no Catholics still reside near the old urban churches and schools. . . . Yet there are plenty of other places where today's Catholic immigrants (Hispanic mostly) have taken up residence in neighborhoods formerly inhabited by yesterday's immigrants (Irish, Italians, Poles, etc.). The sensitive question is whether these established, assimilated, middle-class, suburban Catholics will be willing to support the education of Hispanic Catholic children living in the inner city.

We believe the answer is "yes." Our optimism is rooted in the second lesson learned from Wichita: that Catholics will indeed open their pocketbooks to support Catholic schools—at least, in order to educate Catholics. For it is the *religious* mission of these schools that motivates parishioners to tithe. As Rev. Ken VanHaverbeke, the pastor of St. Joseph's in downtown Wichita, explains, "People see that the Catholic school is a very good vehicle for passing on their faith." Thus it's not surprising that our survey found that the attribute Catholics most associate with Catholic parochial schools is "developing moral values and discipline."

Many Catholic education leaders say they can't compete with "free" charter schools, even when recruiting Catholic families. Here's the solution: Make Catholic schools free, too.

Catholic Education for Non-Catholics

If the Church were starting anew and designing its education system from scratch, it would likely place its schools near today's concentrations of Catholic parishioners. That's certainly where it's building new schools—in the suburbs, where many Catholics now dwell. But today's urban Catholic schools are a legacy of an earlier time when immigrant Catholics lived in the city and wanted their children to get a parochial education. As [urban-Catholic-school-reform specialist Scott W.] Hamilton notes, most of these families decamped to the suburbs in the 1960s and '70s. The result was the slow decline of so many urban parishes—and so many parish schools. But time and again the Church renewed its commitment to keep these schools open anyway to serve the poor children who now lived in these communities. And many studies have shown that the schools served these children well.

Thus America still finds itself with hundreds of Catholic schools in its inner cities, where they mainly serve poor non-Catholics, particularly African Americans. Now, however, the Church is saying—perhaps whispering—that it can no longer afford to foot the growing bill. (The financial hit from the recent sex-abuse scandals was the last straw.)

Priorities of Catholic Parishioners

Catholic parishioners have been willing to help to a point, but our survey shows that about six in ten Catholics now view "working with economically disadvantaged students" as the domain of public schools. And while they like the idea of keeping urban Catholic schools open, they rank that goal below many other social priorities, particularly that of caring for the poor and sick through traditional charities and Catholic hospitals.

If parishioners don't rate educating poor youngsters a high priority and the Church can't afford it, who will save these schools now?

Our case studies offer some tantalizing insights. One is that philanthropists will respond to the call if convinced that Catholic schools are providing an excellent education for low-income children. So it was in Memphis, where the Jubilee Schools received massive donations from non-Catholics impressed by their educational results. Philanthropists in other cities could and should follow suit—and other Catholic school systems should be transparent about their educational outcomes so as to attract social investors and benefactors to their cause. (Secrecy about such matters—absolutely archaic in the NCLB [No Child Left Behind, the federal education program implemented during the George W. Bush administration] era—plagues most U.S. private schools, including but not limited to Catholic schools.)

Second, though this flies in the face of school choice orthodoxy, public support for Catholic schools in the form of vouchers is no panacea. The urban schools of Milwaukee, home to the nation's largest voucher program, continue to decline. Federally funded vouchers haven't kept the Archdiocese of Washington, D.C., from moving to convert seven of its urban schools into charters in order to tap even more public dollars. In both places, Catholic schools have struggled to compete with private and/or charter schools, demonstrating *inter alia* [among other things] the need for better marketing (Denver shows some promise on that front) and, most importantly, for excellent academics.

Fresh Opportunities

It may be that many archdiocesan systems aren't up to these challenges. Some of them are weary, others broke, and in any case it makes little sense to expect parish priests to run effectively institutions as complex as high-performance schools. This brings us to our third insight: The liveliest signs of energy and strategic thinking in Catholic education today—particularly the kind that benefits non-Catholics—are found in independent networks, such as the Cristo Rey and Nativity schools. They are acting much like charter management organizations like KIPP [Knowledge Is Power Program], Achievement First or Green Dot that play critical roles in boosting the "supply side" of the charter movement by providing high-quality alternatives to monolithic district-run public schools. Supporting their Catholic counterparts and growing more such networks offers another terrific opportunity for philanthropists and, perhaps, the broader public.

What's Worthy of Government Support?

Let's return to a fundamental question: How important is it for urban Catholic schools that serve non-Catholics to remain religious in nature and to continue operating under the Church's aegis? Already they're less "Catholic" than they used to be, as they are no longer staffed by nuns or priests. By and large, they don't seek to proselytize their charges. And rare is the diocese or archdiocese that does a bang-up job of giving its urban schools the educational and fund-raising support they need to survive and thrive.

In principle, we appreciate the argument for keeping these schools Catholic insofar as it's possible. It may well be their encompassing Catholic faith that helps to make them effective. We don't really know what erasing the faith-based approach would mean for the schools' future educational success.

Whether to "Go Charter"

Having said that, we're not convinced that it would be tragic for many of these schools to "go charter," as has been proposed in Washington, D.C., or to sell or lease their buildings to high-quality charter school operators, as has happened nationwide. Ironically, for many urban Catholic schools, or at least for the kids they serve, this may be the best available option—best in the sense that it would continue to make decent educational options available to youngsters who need them. Options without a crucifix on the wall, to be sure, but lots of those kids aren't coming because of the crucifix anyway. They're coming because in these schools they can find safety, competent teachers, a solid curriculum, good behavior, and sound values. When educating low-income, non-Catholic kids, it seems to us, preserving those qualities in a viable school would find greater favor in God's eye than locking the door on an empty building.

In short, public funding is probably necessary to keep these educational options alive. And the price of such funding, at least in many communities and some states (including those with "Blaine Amendments" [provisions in many state constitutions that prohibit direct government aid to religious educational institutions]), is removing the crucifix and (where possible) recycling the school as a high-quality charter.

We wish it could be otherwise, and surely there are a few more places where generous philanthropists, selfless parishioners, or a shower of vouchers could make it so. But we oughtn't kid ourselves into thinking that this will be the norm. These Catholic-schools-for-non-Catholics are essentially serving a public purpose. In a way, they are already "public" schools; it's time that they receive public funds.

Three Recommendations

So let us propose three recommendations of our own . . . :

1. *The Church should heed Wichita's example and embark on a serious campaign to make Catholic education afford-able—even free—for all Catholics.* Such an effort will be particularly significant for America's recent Hispanic immigrants, many of whom live near urban Catholic schools with a rich history of educating children new to our shores. This means asking parishioners to dig deep. It also means being aggressive about revitalizing run-

down, ill-managed parish schools with an eye to making the system as a whole as efficient and effective as possible.

2. *Philanthropists should generously support networks of Catholic schools that operate independently of diocesan structures.* Such networks have the agility and commitment to operate effective schools, including those serving poor non-Catholics. They have the potential to be the "high growth" sector within Catholic education and, if successful, could occupy facilities that would otherwise go to charter schools. University programs that place talented college graduates into needy urban Catholic schools are also worthy of support—just as worthy as the respected (and well-funded) Teach For America.

3. *If closures are inescapable, the Church should either convert those schools to charters or make their facilities available at bargain prices to high-quality charter networks.* Both options are far better for kids than hawking old school buildings to the highest bidder and converting them to condos.

On all these fronts, what's needed most is leadership. We have an opportunity to protect some valuable schools in our neediest neighborhoods. Who will show the way?

"It would be tragic and absurd to help drive these schools out of business by publicly funding student attendance to both public and charter schools, but not to private schools."

Catholic Schools Should Be Saved Through Vouchers and Tax Credits

Matthew Ladner

Matthew Ladner is vice president of research for the Goldwater Institute. In the following viewpoint, he contrasts the state of Catholic school education in Michigan and Arizona, arguing that Catholic education is booming in the latter state because Arizona initiated private school choice programs. Through a series of tax credit initiatives and voucher programs, private school education is subsidized in Arizona, resulting in rising Catholic school enrollment and the building of new Catholic schools in the state.

As you read, consider the following questions:

1. According to a RAND study, are charter schools a bigger threat to private schools or public schools in Michigan?

2. How many Diocese of Detroit schools have closed as of 2007, according to Ladner?

3. How much higher does Ladner report charter school enrollment is in Arizona than in Michigan?

The *Education Next* article "Can Catholic Schools Be Saved?" asks the provocative question: Will charter schools finish off inner-city Catholic private schools? Preliminary evidence suggests that charter schools are actually threatening to help close inner-city Catholic schools. A RAND Corporation study focusing on the impact of charter schools in Michigan found that private schools were taking a bigger hit from charter school competition than public schools on a student-for-student basis. "Private schools will lose one student for every three students gained in the charter schools," the study concluded.

The Threat Posed by Charter Schools

Ronald Nuzzi, director of the Alliance for Catholic Education Leadership Program at the University of Notre Dame asserted that charter schools "are one of the biggest threats to Catholic schools in the inner city, hands down. How do you compete with an alternative that doesn't cost anything?" Inner-city Catholic schools are in a deep and tragic crisis, especially in Michigan. Sadly, Michigan's constitution essentially forbids private school choice of any sort, and the Diocese of Detroit has witnessed a 20 percent decline in enrollment since 2002 and currently faces another round of school closures. Overall, 29 Diocese of Detroit schools have already closed.

Ironically, many of the best charter schools, such as the KIPP [Knowledge Is Power Program] academies, drew inspira-

School Choice Is Good for Catholic Schools

Not every qualified student will choose a Catholic school, but it is likely that many will. We already know how the EITC [educational improvement tax credit] has helped our schools; SB 1 [Senate Bill 1, a school choice bill in Pennsylvania] will help many current Catholic school families and will allow even more children a chance to get a Catholic education. Having more students in our classrooms is good news for our schools; more students will help us keep our schools vibrant and available to parents.

"Q & A: Why Should Catholics Support School Choice?,"
Viewpoint: Newsletter of the Pennsylvania
Catholic Conference, *Spring 2011.*

tion from Catholic school practices. Research by Stanford economist Caroline Hoxby has demonstrated that charter schools have spurred a positive competitive response from adjacent public schools. Other research, including a Goldwater Institute study by Lew Solomon and Pete Goldschmidt have shown that students enrolling in charter schools make larger achievement gains than their public school peers.

Saving Urban Catholic Schools

A fully scaled system of charter schools for inner-city areas may represent an existential threat to inner-city Catholic schools already struggling with the loss of religious staff and the movement of parishioners to the suburbs. In many inner-city areas, Catholic schools have been the only high-performing schools for decades. Catholic schools have an especially strong record in successfully educating disadvantaged students and sending them on to college. It would be tragic and absurd to help drive these schools out of business by publicly funding student attendance to both public and charter schools, but not to private schools.

Writing in the latest issue of the *Catholic Education*, I detailed a more hopeful example than Michigan: Arizona. Total charter school enrollment is 12.5 percent higher in Arizona than in Michigan, despite the fact that Michigan's population is far larger than Arizona's. Arizona, however, has two factors working for it that Michigan does not. Arizona has both a growing student population and private school choice programs (two tax credit programs and two voucher programs).

Catholic Education in Arizona

Catholic education is anything but wilting in Arizona. Between 2004 and 2006, schools in the Diocese of Phoenix saw a two percent increase in enrollment against a national decline. Two new Catholic schools opened in the 2006–2007 school year, with four more scheduled to open. Marybeth Mueller, superintendent of Catholic schools for the Diocese of Phoenix, stated that the tax credit program has been "critical to keeping financially struggling families in the Catholic school system."

Arizona private school attendance has increased outside of the Catholic schools as well. Despite the opening of hundreds of charter schools, the percentage of Arizona children attending private schools increased by 23 percent between 1991 and 2003, according to the National Center for Education Statistics.

Parents must pay public school taxes even if they do their fellow taxpayers the service of placing [their children] in a private school at their own expense. If parents decide to seek a [private] education . . . for their children, they effectively pay twice—once when they pay taxes, another when they pay tuition and fees.

Both tax credits and school vouchers can reduce this double payment penalty, expanding access to private schooling. In the process, competition will improve the performance of public schools by expanding competition for students, and (in states like Arizona) reduce public school overcrowding.

Arizona and Michigan have both enjoyed the large benefits of charter schools. The starkly different trends in private schooling suggest strongly that choice supporters must redouble their efforts on the private choice side.

Periodical and Internet Sources Bibliography

The following articles have been selected to supplement the diverse views presented in this chapter.

Peter Applebome	"The Promise and Costs of Charters," *New York Times*, March 9, 2011.
Jacob Berkman	"Orthodox Grapple with Charter School Concept," *Jewish Chronicle*, March 9, 2009.
Mary Budd	"Charter Schools Reveal How to Step Out of the Box," *Bangor Daily News* (Maine), February 8, 2011.
Economist	"Schools and Religion: God and Times Tables," May 13, 2010.
Javier C. Hernandez	"Hurdles for a Plan to Turn Catholic Classrooms into Charter Schools," *New York Times*, February 15, 2009.
Theola Labbé	"Church Decides to Convert 7 Schools," *Washington Post*, November 6, 2007.
Jennifer Medina	"Success and Scrutiny at Hebrew Charter School," *New York Times*, June 24, 2010.
Jessica Meyers	"Charter Schools with Ties to Religious Groups Raise Fears About State Funds' Use," *Dallas Morning News*, November 22, 2010.
Rmuse	"Vouchers from God: The Religious Right's Plot Against Public Education," PoliticusUSA, May 12, 2011. http://www.politicususa.com.
Matthew Rousu	"Benefits of School Vouchers Outweigh the Negative Aspects," *Patriot-News* (Pennsylvania), February 8, 2011.

CHAPTER 3

Do Online Charter Schools Work?

Chapter Preface

One of the fastest growing trends in education is online charter schools, also known as cyber charters or virtual charters, which allow students to use the Internet to receive K–12 instruction. Like other charter schools, they are publicly funded and must meet several state and federal requirements. Students enrolled in online charters are provided with instruction, such as online lectures and tutoring, as well as supplies, which may include a personal computer and an Internet connection. Many schools offer some in-person interaction for students, such as field trips or extracurricular activities. Students can choose from several curricula or programs. They must also take all state exams, and receive an official diploma upon fulfilling the criteria for graduation. Thousands of US K–12 students have enrolled in online charter schools since their development.

According to scholar and educator Rob Darrow, the concept of online learning first emerged not long after the creation of the Internet in 1969. At that time, the first Internet nodes were limited to several West Coast universities: University of California at Berkeley, Stanford, and University of California at Santa Barbara. By 1973 a British college, known as the Open University, began to adapt television and Internet technology to enroll and educate students over long distances. In 1982 the Computer Assisted Learning Center (CALC) was established in Rindge, New Hampshire, as an adult learning center that used computers for instructional purposes. CALC's founder, Margaret Morabito, realized the potential of the Internet for education and turned CALC into an online learning center, focusing in particular on providing distance learning for adults using developing Internet technologies. By 1985 CALC's online adult learning center was functioning on a limited basis; a year later, CALC's first Tutoring Center went live.

CALC then founded the QuantamLink Community College, which featured virtual classroom instruction for college students.

A number of educators were excited by the potential of online learning technology for K–12 education. In 1991 Minnesota passed the first charter school law; a year later, City Academy, the nation's first charter school, opened in St. Paul. That same year, California became the second state to pass a charter school law.

The first online charter school was opened in Riverside County, California, in 1994. Choice 2000 utilized audio broadcast over the Internet for teaching K–12 instruction. Later that same year, Utah established the state's first online charter school. These schools were followed by online charter schools in Massachusetts and Florida. As more Americans became familiar with Internet technology, the idea of online education programs evolved into a popular and practical option for states looking into innovative approaches to education reform. For many parents, educators, and policy makers, online charters are a viable way to help children in isolated areas or with special educational needs.

Today online charters are one of the fastest growing segments of US education. The Center for Education Reform lists 216 online charters in its National Charter School Directory. The following chapter considers the popularity of online charters and investigates recent controversies over funding and academic performance concerning these schools.

> *"Virtual learning has become feasible for a growing number of students because of technological innovations and sophisticated instructional delivery programs."*

Online Charter Schools Expand Options and Benefit Students

Michael Van Beek

Michael Van Beek is the director of education policy at the Mackinac Center for Public Policy in Michigan. In the following viewpoint, he examines the growing educational trend toward online learning, noting that it can meet the needs of students who do not thrive in traditional classroom settings. Van Beek also asserts that online learning offers more courses and programs and more flexibility with scheduling that can be tailored to a particular student's needs. He assesses the success of existing online charters, pointing out that studies have shown that they are as successful or more successful than traditional public school settings.

As you read, consider the following questions:

1. According to a 2009 US Department of Education study, how do students in online learning conditions perform in relation to those receiving face-to-face instruction?

2. How do advanced placement students from the Florida Virtual School perform in relation to conventional public school students, according to the Florida TaxWatch Center for Educational Performance and Accountability?

3. How many South Korean students use MegaStudy.net, one of the country's largest online tutoring services, according to the *New York Times*?

Schools are offering more virtual learning options for a number of reasons. First, virtual learning can meet the needs of students who struggle to succeed in the conventional classroom setting. Second, virtual classes let students access courses and programs that might not be available to them in their local school. Third, virtual learning provides flexibility; students do not need to adhere to a traditional school schedule to complete their work and earn a diploma.

Virtual learning may not be for every student. Some students don't have the time-management skills, personal motivation or adult support to succeed in a virtual environment. Others may simply prefer the traditional approach. Nevertheless, virtual learning has become feasible for a growing number of students because of technological innovations and sophisticated instructional delivery programs.

Evaluations of Virtual Learning

This is promising, since the most recent research suggests that online and blended learning can actually boost student achievement. The U.S. Department of Education in 2009 released the findings from a meta-analysis of empirical research on online learning conducted between 1996 and 2008. This meta-analysis screened more than 1,100 studies on the topic and reviewed studies of both blended learning and full-time online courses. Based on the studies that met their rigorous methodological criteria, they concluded, "[O]n average, students in online learning conditions performed better than those receiving face-to-face instruction."

The authors of that study also noted, however, that most of the studies that met their criteria came from higher education, professional training or adult learning courses. Only five of the virtual learning studies that met their criteria dealt specifically with K-12 education. For this reason, the authors were reluctant to draw wide-ranging conclusions. Whether virtual learning can produce superior results for all students on average in a K-12 environment is yet to be completely determined, but there is research that suggests it can at least hold its own against traditional instruction.

In 2001, Cathy Cavanaugh, an associate professor at the University of Florida and an experienced researcher of online learning, published a meta-analysis of distance-learning technologies. Using 19 studies that met her research quality standards, Cavanaugh found no statistically significant difference in student performance between face-to-face instruction and that provided in a virtual environment.

The Case of Florida Virtual School

Results from Florida Virtual School [FLVS]—the nation's largest state "virtual school"—also suggest that students are learning well online. This virtual school provides a variety of online learning courses that are accepted for credit in Florida school districts, and any student in Florida is eligible to enroll. In 2007, the Florida TaxWatch Center for Educational Performance and Accountability, a nonprofit research group, compared the test scores of students taking Advanced Placement [AP] courses through FLVS with those taking the courses in Florida's brick-and-mortar school districts. The average AP

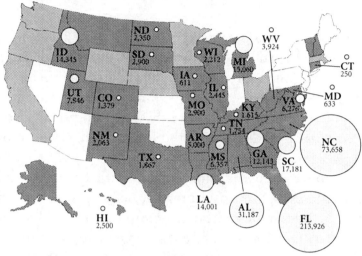

States with State Virtual Schools or State-Led Online Initiatives

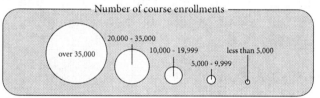

Number of course enrollments

over 35,000   20,000 - 35,000   10,000 - 19,999   less than 5,000   5,000 - 9,999

States with state virtual schools (dark gray) or state-led online learning initiatives (light gray). Circles and numbers indicate number of course enrollments in state virtual schools.

TAKEN FROM: Evergreen Education Group, *Keeping Pace with K–12 Online Learning: An Annual Review of Policy and Practice (2010)*, 2010.

test score through FLVS in 2005 was 14 percent higher than the average AP test score in conventional public school districts and 11 percent higher than the average AP test score for all Florida students, including private and independent schools. In 2006, the FLVS average AP score increased, while the other scores fell. The FLVS AP students scored on average 22 percent higher than Florida's conventional public school students and 19 percent higher than all Florida students.

South Korea

Another example of a potential positive outcome from the increased use of virtual learning comes from South Korea. South Korean parents often hire private tutors to help their children prepare for competitive university entrance exams. Generally, the wealthiest parents could afford the best tutors, and all else being equal, the students with the best tutoring were more likely to get into a university.

But through online learning, more South Korean parents can now afford high-quality tutoring, helping to reduce the disparity between rich and poor. According to the *New York Times*, MegaStudy.net, one of South Korea's largest online tutoring services, serves nearly 3 million students and charges only about $30 to $40 per course—a fraction of the cost of traditional private tutoring.

Benefits for Teachers

Despite these low fees, teachers in virtual learning environments can earn good money, since there are few limits on how many students they can serve online. Rose Lee and Woo Hyeong-cheol, the most popular private tutors in the country, are well-paid celebrities in South Korea: Lee earns about $7 million tutoring English, while Hyeong-cheol earns $4 million tutoring math. Almost all of their income flows from online revenues; Hyeong-cheol, for instance, tutors about 50,000 students through the Internet. Both Lee and Hyeong-cheol make salaries competitive with the highest-paid professional South Korean baseball players.

> "We know that too much 'screen time' isn't good for kids; now we expect them to do the majority of their educational activities online?"

Online Charters May Fail Students and Reduce Public School Funding

Weintana Abraha

Weintana Abraha is a reporter for the Atlanta Post. *In the following viewpoint, she explores the heated debate surrounding online charter schools. Critics of online charters argue that these schools do not provide a well-rounded, quality education; drain essential funding away from traditional public schools; and do not provide enough socialization for students. Abraha notes that with studies showing some level of academic success for online charters, the debate will continue to rage concerning the future of online learning.*

As you read, consider the following questions:

1. How many US states have charter schools, according to Abraha?

2. How many virtual or cyber charter schools does the author say exist in the United States?

3. According to Abraha, what percentage of Pennsylvania Cyber Charter School students go to a two- or four-year college?

The one commonality educators have regarding online schools, particularly cyber charter schools, is a passionate opinion about their contribution to American education. The politics and turf war between traditional (also known as brick-and-mortar) and online schools have made it difficult to collect public, nonpartisan data on virtual charter schools and online education in general.

The Rise of Online Charter Schools

Currently, 39 states and the District of Columbia have charter schools; of the nearly 5,000 charter schools across the country, 217 are virtual or cyber charter schools. Additionally, there are hundreds of private and university-run online high schools along with a growing number of brick-and-mortar schools adding online components to their teaching.

Critics have two primary complaints: that it is difficult, if not impossible, for virtual schools to provide quality education. An Arizona State University study of virtual schools critiqued Knowledge Universe, a conglomerate of online schools. "The curriculum is not interesting and it promotes a one-size-fits-all approach. The instruction is mechanical and the system does not encourage creativity." Advocates counter that cyber charter education is the solution for students who are under-stimulated, overlooked, or face disciplinary and/or health issues that traditional schools are ill equipped to deal with. "We get both ends of it: kids who have failed out and kids pursuing careers while going to high school," says Fred Miller, a communications coordinator with the Pennsylvania Cyber Charter School [PCCS]. Moriah Conant, a PCCS sophomore agrees. "I like charter in general because they offer flexibility and it's a great opportunity to have a good education and still do other things like ballet or professional sports."

Additionally, cyber schools must meet the same standards as their brick-and-mortar counterparts. "All the [cyber charter] schools have to take the standardized PSSA (Pennsylvania System of School Assessment) tests and meet Adequate Yearly Progress (AYP) under the No Child Left Behind Act," explains Miller. "If you don't make AYP, you're labeled a failing school." Accredited non-charter schools online must have profiles with education watchdog groups in their region.

The Issue of Funding

Another charge against charter and cyber charter education is that they drain essential funding away from public school districts. In a recent *Kansas City Star* article, Pennsylvania's Auditor General, Jack Wagner—a one-time proponent of charter schools—discussed plans to halt new funding for charter and cyber charter education, citing the schools as a hurdle to efficient public school spending. Wagner said, "I cannot turn a blind eye to the inefficiencies in the way charter and cyber-charter schools are funded in Pennsylvania." But according to the Center for Education Reform's website, cyber charter (and charter) schools often receive 66–75% of state funding per student versus public school districts.

Socialization Concerns

Online educators, however, say that they are providing the best possible educational experiences for students who are often overlooked in mainstream public schools—minorities, children in poorer urban and rural communities, and special needs students. Resources include textbooks (or digital texts in some cases) as well as school-provided computer and Internet for every student. Online school communities even work at building non-computer social ties: "One of the myths about cyber is that they don't get enough socialization. They get plenty of socialization," says Miller. "One of the trends we've fostered in the last few years is more face-to-face stuff: regional offices where tutoring is offered; field trips all year; we have a department called FamilyLink that set up trips, outings with families to get together to see each other."

Many students even continue friendships with students outside the online education community. Says Conant, "I do have friends from church who go to brick-and-mortar schools."

But is the moderate amount of social interaction enough to assuage the concerns? "Already, we have too many kids who lack appropriate social skills when they reach school age, and the problem generally only worsens as they get older," says Corinne Gregory, president and founder of SocialSmarts, a nationally recognized program for teaching social skills. "We know that too much 'screen time' isn't good for kids; now we expect them to do the majority of their educational activities online?"

Gregory believes that even the small interaction provided by cyber schools does not address the needs of developing teenagers. "Even the best technology is no good substitute for in-person interaction," she said. "Giving someone your attention, looking them in the eyes, speaking *to* them instead of away, learning how to take turns, communication, and sharing ideas and cooperating—all these things are difficult to 'simulate' online, and it is still, at best, just a 'simulation.'"

Dr. Wendy H. Weiner agrees. As a principal of a small high school in South Florida, she said that her school had to discontinue an online program they had for students, which occupied half of the school day, after seeing the day-to-day struggles of the students during the two-year duration of the program. "I had found that students need to see the face-to-face reactions of working with peers and the teacher," she said.

"The other issue is that the intonation of what is written over the Internet is not necessarily what was meant by the author."

The ultimate question on this debate remains: What is best for students and for public education as a whole?

A Record of Success Fuels Debate

It seems that these alternative institutions can claim some amount of success. Pennsylvania Cyber Charter School's average ACT and SAT scores (22.4 and 1515, respectively) are higher than both the state and national averages (21.9 & 1473 for Pennsylvania; 21 & 1509 for the country). Seventy percent of PA Cyber Charter School students matriculate to a 2- or 4-year college.

If more online educational institutions follow the cyber model, it will continue to fuel the never-ending debate on the state of education. Certainly, more attention must be paid to this new movement to ensure it fulfills its promise to public school students, particularly the ones on the fringe. And though opinions of online schools waver between elation, skepticism, and downright anger, there is no doubt that virtual education will not easily or quietly go away anytime soon.

> "The existing [educational] offerings are making life better for hundreds of thousands of kids. But we're a long way from widespread access to genuinely innovative educational practices."

Online Charters Are Innovative and Effective

Katherine Mangu-Ward

Katherine Mangu-Ward is a senior editor at Reason *magazine. In the following viewpoint, she traces the types of online charter programs, contending that they are becoming popular because they fit the needs of many students better than traditional schools can. Mangu-Ward outlines some of the emerging innovative approaches in online charter education, including hybrid approaches that offer students the benefits of online programs with a level of personal attention and socialization with their peers. She observes that online charters hold tremendous potential for students and the future of education.*

As you read, consider the following questions:

1. According to the Kaiser Family Foundation, how many hours a day do American kids spend in front of a screen?

2. How many public school students does Mangu-Ward report are enrolled in online classes?

3. According to the author, how many states allow full-time online programs?

I know a 3-year-old who's a master of online multitasking. Give him an iPhone, and he'll cheerfully chat you up while watching YouTube cartoons or playing an alphabet game. In 2010, toddlers start consuming digital information not long after they've started consuming solid food.

Now take that kid, tack on a handful of years, and drop him into a classroom. A child who was perfectly content with a video stream, an MP3, and a chat flowing past him is suddenly ordered to sit still, shut up, and listen while a grown-up scrawls on a blackboard and delivers a monologue. And school is even worse for the older girls down the hall. The center of their universe is on social networking and chat sites, so spending six hours a day marooned in a building with no WiFi is akin to water torture. The same preteen who will happily while away hours playing Scrabble with her friends on Facebook dreads each Thursday afternoon, when she will be forced to laboriously write out a list of spelling words in silence alongside two dozen peers.

During the last 30 years, the per-student cost of K–12 education has more than doubled in real dollars, with no academic improvement to show for it. Meanwhile, everything the Internet touches gets better: listening to music on iTunes, shopping for shoes at Zappos, exchanging photos on Flickr.

Playing to Their Strengths

Even with school hours off-line, kids are logging plenty of computer time. A January [2010] study by the Kaiser Family Foundation found that kids spend an average of 7.5 hours a day in front of a screen. The knee-jerk response is to lament those lost hours and hatch schemes to pry the kids' hands from their keyboards. But that's the wrong approach. If you can't beat 'em, join 'em: Let kids stare at a computer screen until their eyeballs fall out, but add more educational material to the mix.

A growing number of kids and their parents are figuring out ways to sneak schoolwork online. More than 1 million public school students are enrolled in online classes, up from about 50,000 a decade ago. In Florida, nearly 80,000 kids take classes in the state-sponsored Florida Virtual School. Virtual charter school companies such as K12 Inc. provide full-time online education to 70,000 students in 25 states. Hundreds of small, innovative companies are springing up, vying to combine learning with the power of the Internet. Nationwide, 17 percent of high school students report having taken an online course for school in the last year; another 12 percent say they took a class on their own time. Harvard Business School professor Clayton Christensen, co-author of *Disrupting Class*, a seminal 2008 book about online education, estimates that half of all high school courses in the United States will be consumed over the Internet by 2019.

But the commercial Internet has already been around for a decade and a half. As the 3-year-old with the iPhone might whine from the back seat of the minivan: Why aren't we there yet?

School in the Sunshine State

Online education's biggest success to date is the Florida Virtual School (FLVS). Founded in 1997, FLVS was the first public statewide online education program in the country.

Founder Julie Young had snagged a $200,000 "Break the Mold" grant from the state of Florida to experiment with online learning. In the early days, as she traveled the state selling the idea to local districts, the reception was muted. "People were sitting there with arms folded and saying, 'You've got to be kidding me,'" recalls the friendly, carefully manicured Young, who had previously worked as a teacher and technology adviser in the state's public schools.

With the election of Jeb Bush in 1998, Young found herself working under a governor with a serious interest in education reform. With Bush's support, legislation expanding the virtual school gave the program a unique advantage: Rather than allowing school officials to be the arbiters of who gets to go online and how, the law said any Florida student who wants to take an FLVS course online must be allowed to do so. The students themselves—not preoccupied guidance counselors, budget-conscious principals, or any other gatekeepers—decided whether to give the virtual school a try.

A Complement to Traditional Public Schools

As the Harvard education scholar Paul Peterson put it in his 2010 book *Saving Schools*, "Much like an Everglades alligator, Young took a quiet, underwater approach." At a time when Gov. Bush and his cadre of education reformers were regularly butting heads with the educational establishment, Young went out of her way not to antagonize teachers' unions or disparage traditional schools. "From day one, what we tried to do was design FLVS so that it was not competitive with the schools, but complementary," she says. Her pedagogical philosophy is noncontroversial—with a few exceptions, the curriculum is typical of the stuff Florida students would get in a traditional classroom—and she is studiedly nonpolitical. The courses offered by FLVS are supplemental; the virtual school cannot grant degrees on its own. Nearly every student remains enrolled in a full-time program at a physical school. The funding formula adopted by the state takes only a fraction of the annual per-student cost from their local school, and FLVS gets paid only when students successfully complete the course.

Young doesn't use the language of reform or revolution. Instead she talks about "doing what's right for kids." Yet Florida Virtual School's model is, in its own way, revolutionary. The school employs 1,200 accredited, nonunion teachers, who are available by phone or e-mail from 8 A.M. to 8 P.M., seven days a week. Kids take what they want, when they want. The academic results are more than respectable. FLVS boasts that kids in advanced placement [AP] courses—39 percent of whom are minority students—score an average of 3.05 out of 5, compared with a state average of 2.49 for students in off-line public school classes. FLVS students also beat state averages in reading and math at all grade levels, with 87 percent of eighth graders receiving at least a passing score on the state standardized test in math, compared with 60 percent statewide. Even critical studies of educational achievement in Florida's online courses find that the results are as good as or better than state averages on virtually every measure.

Picking Fights

Not all of the major players in online education have opted for the stealthy alligator approach. K12 Inc., one of the largest private providers nationwide, doesn't mind picking political fights. One of its founders is [Ronald] Reagan administration secretary of education Bill Bennett, an outspoken conservative. (He resigned from the school's leadership in 2005 after some intemperate remarks about the alleged links between abortion, race, and crime.) While FLVS was sneaking up on the Sunshine State's educational establishment, K12 Inc. started showing up all over the country in 2000 with a bullhorn.

Unlike FLVS, K12 provides full-time instruction. That means students from kindergarten through 12th grade can do their entire school year online. While the curriculum isn't particularly innovative, the model is potentially far more disruptive than a program like FLVS. K12 takes children and teenagers out of school and away from traditional teacher-student relationships. The company has some partnerships with traditional public schools, but K12 primarily works by helping charter schools in states with lenient laws go virtual, accepting kids (and the money they bring with them) from all over the state.

Conflicts over Funding

In the zero-sum world of education dollars, that approach means that state education bureaucrats generally don't show up at K12's virtual door with welcoming tater tot casseroles. In 2003 Wisconsin's Northern Ozaukee School District was experiencing declining enrollment and hoped that bringing in a virtual charter might attract students (and their per-pupil spending allocations) from around the state. This worked brilliantly, with 500 students signing up for the virtual charter school from all over the state in the program's first year. The district and K12 split the $5,000 that came with each kid, and everyone was happy. Well, everyone except the administrators and teachers in the districts losing enrollment dollars to the experiment in online learning. The conflict exploded in January 2004 with a lawsuit brought by the teachers' union and the elected state superintendent. State Sen. John Lehman (D-Racine), who heads his chamber's education committee, accused private education companies of "profiteering off of kids."

The result was a compromise that neutered virtual education in Wisconsin. K12 could continue to operate, but it could enroll students only from the physical district where the charter school was located—essentially stopping the Internet at the

131

county line. And enrollment was capped at 5,250 students. For good measure, Wisconsin announced plans to create an FLVS-like state-sponsored virtual academy, which will compete with K12 on lopsided terms and, unlike in Florida, be firmly under the control of the education bureaucracy.

Unions Fight Back

The National Education Association, the country's main teachers' union, takes a hard line on virtual charters such as K12. "There also should be an absolute prohibition against the granting of charters for the purpose of homeschooling, including online charter schools that seek to provide home-schooling over the Internet," says the organization's official policy statement on charter schools. "Charter schools whose students are in fact homeschoolers, and who may rarely if ever convene in an actual school building, disregard the important socialization aspect of public education, do not serve the public purpose of promoting a sense of community, and lend themselves too easily to the misuse of public funds and the abuse of public trust." But analog unions can't stave off online education for digital natives forever, and state-run virtual academies like FLVS—rather than virtual charters like K12—make it easier to control the pace of change.

Similar battles have been fought in Oregon, where the state teachers' union declared last year [in 2009] that resisting another full-time virtual charter company, the Baltimore-based Connections Academy, would be its top priority. "You'd think among all the kids in Oregon there are some other pressing issues," says Barbara Dreyer, CEO of Connections, which runs one Oregon school and dozens of others across the country. When 2009 began, the state legislature had already obliged the union by capping enrollment for virtual schools and mandating that kids do work under the eyes of physically present teachers. Yet union support for funding and expanding the state's Oregon Virtual School District (which has been slow to attract enrollment) remained strong, with union members citing the existence of the government-run academy as sufficient to meet online education needs in the state.

Says Dreyer: "Many states say, 'We hate the whole thing with these for-profit providers. We should just do it ourselves.' But with the exception of FLVS, nobody has been able to do it. It's complicated; it takes capital. It's tough to do it from scratch. They don't have expertise. It's particularly tough in these times when there is no money."

The Case of Indiana

Something analogous happened four years ago in Indiana, where the charter school law seemed to authorize the creation of full-time online schools. K12 launched a program and started recruiting students. Even though the legislative session was over for the year, when opponents of online education got wind of the new venture they executed some special maneuvers to insert language into the budget bill to kill the virtual charters. While a hybrid model did get up and running, it was on a far smaller scale than originally intended, leaving most of the interested parents and kids out in the cold. This year, with the demand for online education still growing, the union supported the creation of a 200-person pilot program for the state education department to run its own virtual academy.

In its 2010 legislative program, the Indiana State Teachers Association claims to support virtual schools. That is, as long as the programs adhere to nearly all of the criteria that define traditional schools, including class size, seat time, teacher licensing, grading mechanisms, and the physical location and conditions for testing. They can't open their programs to homeschooled kids, and they can't spend more than 5 percent of their budgets on administrative costs.

What Is Blended Learning?

The simplest definition of blended learning is that it is an educational practice that combines elements of online and brick-and-mortar teaching and learning, but this definition is not nearly comprehensive. The International Association for K–12 Online Learning (iNACOL) defines blended learning as having three dimensions that demarcate the concept:

1. Scope may be a "blended learning program" or a "blended course";

2. Blended learning combines two delivery modes of instruction, online and face-to-face; the communication in both modes is enhanced by a learning management system;

3. The role of the teacher is critical, as blended learning requires a transformation of instruction as the teacher becomes a learning facilitator; instruction involves increased interaction between student-and-instructor, student-to-content and student-to-student.

Although "blended learning" is a noun, the term "blended" can also be an adjective that describes different units of education.

"Emerging Issues and Trends," Keeping Pace with K–12 Online Learning: An Annual Review of Policy and Practice, *Evergreen Education Group, 2010. www.mivu.org.*

Teachers' unions, consistently among the biggest donors to U.S. election campaigns, are incredibly powerful. The National Education Association can buy and sell elections, but a continuous flow of membership dues will be tougher to come by if online education blooms.

Make New Friends

Politics aren't the only reason online education is coming to the masses at the speed of a 14k modem. Cultural resistance is strong as well. Parents and politicians fret about the consequences of creating a nation of lonely nerds with Google tans.

Socialization looms large in discussions of online education, but the worriers may be missing the point. For one thing, kids are already doing much of their socializing on their screens. That hasn't brought sports, clubs, summer camp, or neighborhood activities to an end, and neither will online education.

More important, it's not clear that the kind of socialization we're currently offering kids in schools is doing them any favors. Even in schools where the quality of education is decent, enthusiastically partaking in it can make you a mockable nerd, even a target for daily brutalization. The problem is worse among minority populations at large urban schools. Smart black kids across America are choosing not to speak up in class every day, even when they know the right answer, because it's not worth the social suicide. A large body of social scientific literature investigates this problem, beginning with Signithia Fordham's seminal 1986 paper "Black Students' School Success: Coping with the 'Burden of "Acting White.""" The reasons for the problem remain a topic of heated debate, but the problem itself is well-established: Surveys consistently show that black students worry more than white students that their peers will criticize their academic success.

Addressing Another Social Stigma

While the smartest kids face one set of troubles, the slower kids in the same classes have problems of their own, mutely letting lessons roll by because they're afraid of asking a question and being called stupid. Learning online in the morning and then heading out to play in the park in the afternoons could be a much better alternative for both kinds of kids.

The real issue here isn't socialization but something else. If there is one thing that nearly all American parents have in common, it is the paralyzing fear that they might have to figure out what to do with their children all day, every day, for 12 long years. Michael [B.] Horn, one of the co-authors of *Disrupting Class*, estimates that the number of kids who might learn full time at home tops out at 5 million, a figure based on how many live in family structures that allow for all-day adult supervision. That leaves more than 90 percent of the nation's 55 million schoolage children in need of someplace to go during the day.

The Future of Online Education

One promising idea is a hybrid approach, where kids get the socialization and adult supervision of a shared physical space but consume much of their actual instruction online. Of the million kids already taking classes online, some are just logging in from their bedrooms, but others are taking courses on computers in community centers or gyms or heading out to the strip-mall outposts of private tutoring companies.

Such hybrids are springing up around the country. Rocketship Education in San Jose, California, brings at-risk elementary students together in a safe, colorful, trailer-like modular space, with a small staff to keep an eye on the kids while they do lessons online. Dropout recovery programs such as AdvancePath Academics catch kids who have fallen out of the system. Some of these programs, in which the content is administered primarily online, give kids physical spaces to learn in shopping malls. Kids in mentoring programs such as Group Excellence are offered a choice: They can opt for after-school tutoring in a physical space with free pizza, or take advantage of 24-hour support to do the same work on an iPhone, netbook, desktop, or even a Nintendo, whenever they want.

State governments spend between $10,000 and $15,000 annually on each of the nation's 55 million schoolkids, making primary and secondary education a $1 trillion market. Under ordinary circumstances, that kind of money attracts entrepreneurs. But the uncertainties of politics, the powerful opposition of the teachers' unions, and the astonishing technological backwardness of the education establishment discourage would-be entrepreneurs and, perhaps more importantly, potential investors.

New and Innovative Approaches Are Emerging

In the 2010 annual letter from his charitable foundation—the biggest in the United States, with a $33 billion endowment—Bill Gates listed online education as one of his top priorities. "Online learning can be more than lectures," he wrote. "Another element involves presenting information in an interactive form, which can be used to find out what a student knows and doesn't know." Hundreds of smaller contenders are proliferating, trying to figure out ways to exploit the new medium and answer concerns about what a nation of online learners might look like. Carnegie Learning uses artificial intelligence techniques to customize math learning to the individual. The Online School for Girls creates and administers advanced courses geared to female learning styles. The list is as large and diverse as the iPhone app store and growing every day.

Internet access isn't a barrier anymore. The digital divide has essentially closed. A 2009 Pew Research Center report found that 93 percent of Americans between the ages of 12 and 17 are online. Computers are cheap, and they're getting cheaper every day. Textbooks are expensive, and they always have been. There's a point not too far off where the price of a decent laptop and the price of a single hardback biology textbook will converge. Books full of non-hyperlinked text already must seem like a cruel joke to the congenitally connected. The virtual charter school company Connections Academy supplies its 20,000 full-time students with computers as part of the package.

Adults who weren't weaned on broadband find the beeps and boops of their computers distracting, but distractions from the computers aren't a problem for kids. Slow brain death from data deficit while they sit still, eyes forward, listening to a one-dimensional lecture that's going too slowly, too quickly, or in the wrong direction altogether is a much more serious threat.

Failing for Success

From the perspective of education reformers and policy wonks, beaten down by a decades-long war of attrition, online education has swept onto the scene with astonishing speed. Paul Peterson, the Harvard education scholar, calls the rate at which the online education sector has grown "breathtaking." But his private-sector counterpart Tom Vander Ark—who helped found the country's first K–12 online school in 1995, served as the executive director of education for the Bill & Melinda Gates Foundation, and now runs a private equity fund focused on education—has a different view. "Coming from the business world, I thought this would all happen fast," he says. "It's frustrating that 15 years later online learning is just beginning to mature."

Until recently, virtual schools have been funded by state education budgets. Now states are increasingly fishing for federal dollars. Sixteen states included an online education component this year when requesting funds from Race to the Top, a federal grant program launched under George W. Bush and expanded under Barack Obama that was designed to bribe states to push toward greater teacher accountability and competition. The first round of funding was awarded in April, and while the inclusion of online education in several of the winning proposals is encouraging, the grants heavily favor top-down, state-run online academies over virtual charters and other bottom-up options.

Vander Ark calls the online component of the Race to the Top finalists' plans "lame." On his blog, he explains: "Given less than optimal policy environments, state v-schools can and do play an important role in supporting blended environments and online options." But "we're a generation behind where we should be in terms of online tools, platforms and options—a state government caused market failure. Where competition is welcomed, we'll see innovation."

A Push for Online Charters

The existing offerings are making life better for hundreds of thousands of kids. But we're a long way from widespread access to genuinely innovative educational practices. Only 28 states allow full-time online programs right now. If you're a kid who lives in New York, you don't have access to any public online programs. In Virginia you have online AP courses, but nothing full time. If you're in California, you have access to full-time programs but not supplemental ones, unless you happen to live in a district that made an independent investment in online learning.

We can't let state legislatures and federal grant programs pick winners. We can't let teachers' unions allow only one version of online education to squeak by. But if online learning keeps growing, when that 3-year-old with the iPhone graduates from high school in 2025, education will be virtually unrecognizable, and thank goodness for that.

> "There are no libraries, cafeterias, play-
> grounds, coaches, janitors, nurses, buses
> or bus drivers—but [virtual schools]
> can cost taxpayers per student as much
> as or more than traditional public
> schools."

Online Charters Are Expensive and Problematic

Carol Pogash

*Carol Pogash is a journalist and author. In the following view-
point, she details the questions some educators and experts have
about the funding of online charter schools. Pogash reports that
many people wonder why online charters receive equal—or in
some cases, more—funding per student than traditional public
schools when they have little overhead. She finds that many experts are concerned about the minimal accountability of many
online charter programs, especially when it comes to funding.*

As you read, consider the following questions:

1. How many students does the author say attend full-time
   virtual charter school nationally?

2. According to the author, what percentage of California's charter schools conduct some or all of their classes online?

3. According to expert Luis Huerta, how do cyber charters compare to traditional public schools when it comes to funding?

Laura Drews has converted a corner of her San Jose dining room into a public school. Every week day, she guides her first-, fifth- and eighth-grade children through their class assignments, delivered through textbooks and desktop computers.

The Drews' unorthodox education is paid for by taxpayers, but created and operated by a for-profit company based in Virginia. The California Virtual Academy at San Mateo is part of an expanding network of virtual public schools, including 10 in the Bay Area, that provide much of the instruction online with the help of a parent.

The schools are a manifestation of the charter school movement, which gives parents and students more choice in public education. Proponents say the virtual schools give students the intimacy of homeschooling while maintaining the structure of a public school. Nationally, there are an estimated 200,000 full-time virtual charter school students, said Susan Patrick, chief executive of the International Association for K–12 Online Learning.

Questions over Funding

Behind the blue screen, however, is a host of unanswered questions about a system that seemingly requires little overhead. There are no libraries, cafeterias, playgrounds, coaches, janitors, nurses, buses or bus drivers—but can cost taxpayers per student as much as or more than traditional public schools.

This year, the San Mateo virtual school attended by the Drews children is expected to receive $5,105 per student in state and federal money—$375 more per student than what children in their authorizing school district of Jefferson Elementary in Daly City are expected to receive, said the district.

K12 Incorporated

The school, California Virtual Academy [CAVA] at San Mateo, is a creation of K12 Incorporated, a publicly traded corporation started in 2000 by Ron Packard, an economist and engineer, and Bill Bennett, the secretary of education under President Ronald Reagan. Initial financing came from Knowledge Universe, a creation of the financier Michael Milken. Milken, who served time in prison in the early 1990s for securities violations, has bought or started dozens of for-profit education companies, including day care centers.

K12 operates virtual schools in 25 states and abroad. It lends students computers, printers, software and books and pays a part of their Internet connection costs. K12 materials include print as well as interactive learning.

K12 signs 3-year-to-10-year management contracts with its charter public schools to provide virtual education. These contracts, according to the company's annual report, "provide the basis for a recurring revenue stream as students progress through successive grades." The company protects its "intellectual property" by having teachers and students sign confidentiality agreements, according to information filed with the Securities and Exchange Commission [SEC].

"A virtual education is expensive," said Katrina Abston, the head of schools for CAVA, and a K12 employee.

The nine K12 California schools share the cost of a 10,000-square-foot office and storage space in Simi Valley. "There's back-end support and computers and the type of curriculum we use is expensive," Abston said. "They make sure we're cutting edge."

More than half the San Mateo virtual academy's budget last year was owed to K12, including $642,304 for management fees to oversee the 900 students in their homes and $2.7 million for instructional materials and technology.

In Pursuit of Profit

Diane Ravitch, a leading educational historian who until recently favored charter schools, is strongly critical of the virtual charter system. Ravitch said the system eliminated "brick-and-mortar schools and it bypasses the unions," mainly for the benefit of for-profit companies.

Twenty percent of California's 872 charter schools now conduct some or all of their classes online. CAVA has 11,000 students in California; 900 are students at CAVA San Mateo, where enrollment is growing at a rate of 20 percent per year, according to K12.

The CAVA curriculum gives "an adult a script on how to teach a student," Drews said. She said she consulted with elementary teachers only about her children's compositions. K12 offers "mastery-based curriculum," with assessment tests that must be passed before a student can move to the next lesson, though at the elementary level those decisions are left to the parents.

High school students can talk to their teachers in voluntary weekly online conferences—but not in person, since their teachers are scattered across the state. They communicate through e-mail and through K12's websites, messaging and internal e-mail system.

Elementary school students learn at their own pace and are graded by their parents. They meet their teachers for a half hour or longer, three or four times a year at a library or church.

CAVA schools rely on the honor system because, short of fingerprint or facial recognition, there is no way to be sure who is tapping at the keyboard. Students in physical education classes—a class that is required by the state—are graded in part on self-reporting of regular exercise.

Evaluating Online Learning

K12 reports that its students test "near state averages," according to documents filed with the SEC. Last year [2009], at CAVA's San Mateo school, 57 percent of students achieved proficiency or above in English; 33 percent were proficient or advanced in math. Nearly 30 percent of the high school students drop out, which is higher than the state average of 24 percent.

Many parents, especially those with younger children, have expressed satisfaction with the curriculum.

"CAVA is beautiful," said Leigh Austin-Schmidt, whose sixth and seventh graders attend school at their home in Pleasanton. "There's a wonderful section on teacher tips, how to prepare for a lesson if I didn't know something."

The San Mateo school attracts families dissatisfied with their public school and seeking a more independent learning environment, flexible hours or more support for students.

Linda Brown said her ninth-grade son, who is in special education, "is doing way better than he would have in public school." But she added that for her fifth-grade daughter, "the social aspect is the thing we miss the most."

On their own, San Jose parents have organized and take turns teaching weekly art, music and science programs at a local church.

A Paper Review

Oversight for California public charter schools falls to the authorizing districts. Although the Jefferson Elementary school district reviews CAVA's curriculum and its budget, it lacks the manpower to verify the records.

"We have to take their word for it," said Enrique Navas, assistant superintendent of business services at the district. "It's a paper review."

Despite the fact that K12 plans to open more schools in the state, Abston, CAVA's head of schools, said all nine California schools operated at a loss.

"K12 provides CAVA a full, turn-key education solution, a complete comprehensive education at a cost less than the average total cost of a student in traditional public schools," Jeff Kwitowski, K12's vice president for public relations, said in an e-mail message. He added that online public schools received about 30 percent less in total financing than traditional schools.

Where Does the Funding Go?

Luis Huerta, an associate professor of education at Teachers College, Columbia University and a nationally recognized scholar on charter schools and school finance who has researched virtual charters for 14 years, disputed that, saying of Kwitowski, "he is unequivocally incorrect."

"Nationally, cyber charters on average receive the equivalent amount of funding as traditional schools," Huerta said.

He added that there was minimal overhead and minimal accountability.

If virtual charter school costs are lower, Huerta said, "then where is the money going?"

"It doesn't add up," he said.

"*The benefits of cyber charter schools are frequently overlooked by traditional school districts.*"

Online Charters Reduce Taxpayer Costs

Commonwealth Foundation

The Commonwealth Foundation is an independent, nonprofit public policy research and educational institute. In the following viewpoint, the authors express their opposition to a plan in Pennsylvania to reduce funding to online charter schools in the state. The Commonwealth Foundation asserts that online schools save taxpayers millions of dollars and that Pennsylvania officials should be focusing on cutting excessive spending in traditional public schools. Nathan Benefield, the director of policy research for the Commonwealth Foundation, argues that traditional public schools may be misusing taxpayer money by spending funds meant for instruction on expensive construction projects.

As you read, consider the following questions:

1. According to the Commonwealth Foundation, how much was Pennsylvania education secretary Gerald L. Zahorchak proposing to spend on online charter school students?

2. How much does Nathan Benefield estimate that cyber schools saved Pennsylvania taxpayers in the 2005–2006 school year?

3. How much did Pennsylvania spend per online charter student before the recent funding cut proposal, according to the authors?

Today, the Commonwealth Foundation issued a response to Pennsylvania education secretary Gerald L. Zahorchak's proposal to reduce funding to the commonwealth's public cyber charter schools.

"We commend Sec. Zahorchak's desire to protect taxpayers from excessive public school spending," said Nathan Benefield, director of policy research for the Commonwealth Foundation, "but he's shooting at the wrong target. Cyber charter schools are saving—not costing—taxpayers millions of dollars. He should be taking aim at the excessive spending in the traditional public school districts, rather than these public schools of choice."

The Proposal

Zahorchak proposed a per-student funding limit of $5,800 for children attending cyber schools. Ostensibly he claims that this limit would protect taxpayers by saving them a total of $25 million—or $4 in property taxes for the average homeowner. "This is a façade," said Benefield. "Cyber schools are already saving taxpayers money. In just the 2005–06 school year, they saved taxpayers more than $146 million."

Cyber schools receive a fraction of the per-student average of $11,500 received by traditional public school districts. Cyber schools receive no funding for facilities, and receive less than 80% what school districts spend on instruction and student services alone. Despite receiving, on average, only $8,300

The "Edifice Complex"

The answer is not that traditional public schools spend too little, but rather, they often spend public money serving the egos of school superintendents and school boards instead of the learning needs of children. Many school districts suffer an "Edifice Complex," putting buildings ahead of teachers and kids. To cure the Edifice Complex, increased public cyber schooling, as demonstrated by Pennsylvania's 11 cyber charter schools, helps children by putting public money where it belongs—in teachers and instructional materials rather than in "Taj Mahal" buildings. Like most private-sector organizations, cyber schools are using the Internet to revolutionize how they serve their clients. School districts would do well to adopt the innovations pioneered in public cyber charter schools. Instead, associations of school boards have decried public cyber schools and called for reducing their funding.

Robert Maranto, Nathan Benefield, and Jason O'Brien,
"Edifice Complex: Where Has All the Money Gone?,"
Commonwealth Foundation, July 2007.

per student, cyber schools must adhere to all of the same accountability measures of traditional public schools—and then some.

"In the name of taxpayer protection, Gov. [Ed] Rendell and Sec. Zahorchak's proposal would likely cost taxpayers more, rather than less," Benefield said. "Reducing the per-student funding by more than 30% would likely force some cyber schools to close down or cut educational services. This will force students back in to high-cost traditional public schools."

The Benefits of Cyber Charters

The benefits of cyber charter schools are frequently overlooked by traditional school districts. "When parents choose to place their children into lower costing cyber schools, they are not only reducing the tax burden on homeowners, but they are helping to alleviate overcrowding and the need for new school construction," said Benefield. "Cybers also help to reduce class size and effectively increase per-pupil spending in district schools."

In a news release, Zahorchak stated, "Pennsylvania taxpayer dollars are not going for their intended use. Simply put, cyber charter schools should be investing their resources in students." But a recent report from the Commonwealth Foundation, titled *Edifice Complex: Where Has All the Money Gone?*, found that cyber schools were much more effective at targeting spending toward students. It was traditional public school districts that were misusing tax dollars designated for education.

The analysis found that over the last 10 years, school district spending on construction and debt increased by a whopping 103%. The research also found that as districts had more money to spend, they spent a relatively higher percentage on construction. The opposite is true of instruction—school districts with more revenues spent a lower percentage on instruction. Benefield said the evidence indicates that when districts are given more resources to spend on education, school boards put more of it toward new buildings, rather than child learning.

Questions over Taxpayer Funding

"There are only two possible explanations," said Benefield, a co-author of *Edifice Complex*. "Either school districts are getting too much money and/or school officials suffer from an 'Edifice Complex' and are misusing taxpayer money—supposedly for instruction—for school construction."

Zahorchak and others also point to cyber schools' fund balances. Cyber schools are exempted from state limits on fund balances because of (1) dramatic enrollment growth (cyber schools may double in size year to year) and (2) school districts are typically late in sending the reduced per-student allocation to the cyber school. Tim Allwein of the Pennsylvania School Boards Association admitted to the *Pittsburgh Tribune-Review* that "districts sometimes refuse to pay for what they see as a flawed system." This is forcing schools to dip into these reserves to cover the costs for children they are educating.

The Commonwealth Foundation also found that 37% of school districts carry fund balances in excess of the 12% limit in state law. "If this limit is neither applied nor enforced for school districts that seem to be hoarding tax collections, there is no justification for imposing it on cyber schools," said Benefield.

"It is unfortunate that Gov. Rendell and Sec. Zahorchak are using the façade of 'protecting taxpayers' to effectively limit public school choices for parents and likely increase taxes on homeowners," said Benefield. "Cyber schools have proven to save taxpayers money, spend the money they receive more efficiently, and serve many individual students better."

> "In contrast to why the public school es-
> tablishment opposes virtual charters,
> many home-school parents are con-
> cerned over the potential for these
> schools to infringe on educational free-
> dom and flexibility."

Online Charter Schools Undermine Homeschooling Efforts

David N. Bass

David N. Bass is a contributing editor of Carolina Journal. *In the following viewpoint, he explores growing concerns that on-line charter schools are threatening home schools by controlling what homeschooled students are taught and luring them back into the public education system. Because online charters are public schools and funded by state and local money, many parents of homeschoolers are enrolling their children in online char-ters and depleting the numbers of homeschooled students in some areas. Bass reports that one of the main concerns is that online charters do not allow faith-based curriculum and materi-als—a requirement that many parents of homeschoolers view as essential to their children's education.*

David N. Bass, "Do Online Charters Threaten Home Schools?," *Carolina Journal*, Sep-tember 12, 2007. Copyright © 2007. All rights reserved. Reproduced by permission.

As you read, consider the following questions:

1. According to the Center for Educational Reform, how many virtual schools were there in 2006?

2. Does North Carolina's charter school law authorize virtual charter schools?

3. What are the concerns expressed by the Idaho Coalition of Home Educators to the Idaho Distance Education Academy, as summed up by the author?

The school-choice movement broadly supports charter schools as a better alternative to the traditional public school system, but many home educators are concerned that online, or "virtual," charter schools are being used to regain control over what home-school students are taught and perhaps lure them back into the public education system.

Virtual charter schools are particularly attractive to homeschoolers because they provide government funds for school materials and allow parents to supervise the learning process at home. In exchange, parents must abide by a government-imposed schedule and restrictions on what curriculum can be taught.

According to Michael Smith, president of the Homeschool Legal Defense Association, an organization dedicated to defending the legal rights of home-school families, many virtual charter school programs are being marketed to homeschoolers.

"There is definitely advertising directed toward the home-school community," he said. "Look what we have for you—we can pay for your books, extracurricular activities, a computer, and all you have to do is sign up."

A Growing Movement

Research gathered by the Center for Education Reform (CER) shows that virtual charters have grown over the last few years, jumping from 89 schools nationally in 2002 to 178 schools in 2006. Virtual schools exist in 19 states and serve more than 93,000 students. More states, including South Carolina, are changing their charter school laws to allow virtual schools.

North Carolina's charter school law does not specifically authorize virtual charter schools, according to Alison Consoletti, director of research for CER. Local school officials and state policy makers have appeared reluctant to authorize both virtual and traditional brick-and-mortar charter schools. Despite repeated attempts over previous legislative sessions to increase the number of charters allowed under state law, the General Assembly has kept the cap at 100 schools.

According to an article in the spring 2005 edition of the *North Carolina Journal of Law & Technology*, some North Carolina school districts have turned down applications for virtual charters in the past. For example, Charlotte-Mecklenburg Schools rejected an attempt to open a virtual charter known as New Connections Academy in 2002, citing "unanswered questions" about the effectiveness of virtual charters.

Like traditional charter schools, virtual charters have faced opposition from the public school establishment. Public school districts are generally not supportive of virtual charters, Consoletti said.

"School districts don't think it's fair that virtual schools receive the same amount of money per pupil because they do not have buildings and therefore don't have the same maintenance [costs] as a traditional school," said Consoletti, pointing to a years-long court battle in Pennsylvania over the 11 virtual charters in the state as evidence of public school opposition.

Recently, a Wisconsin judge ruled against a teachers' union that had filed a lawsuit against the Wisconsin Virtual Academy [WVA], a K-8 virtual charter. The union charged that WVA violated state law by having parents rather than public school instructors educate students, according to the *Milwaukee Jour-*

Virtual Charters Can Pose a Threat to Homeschoolers' Rights

If we don't maintain the distinction between home schools and virtual charter schools, the regulations put on public virtual school students may be put on us. It is ironic, sad, and could be tragic, that we homeschoolers, who started out to maintain our right to educate our children according to our principles and beliefs and not those of the state, could end up under greater government control than families who send their children to conventional public schools. The government could only directly regulate their children while they were attending school, leaving their homes free from government regulation, but it could regulate our children, and us, in our homes.

Larry and Susan Kaseman, "Taking Charge:
Risks Public Virtual Schools Pose to Homeschools,"
Home Education Magazine, *March–April 2008.*

nal Sentinel. The state Department of Public Instruction filed briefs in the case supporting the union's position.

Homeschoolers Are Concerned

In contrast to why the public school establishment opposes virtual charters, many home-school parents are concerned over the potential for these schools to infringe on educational freedom and flexibility.

"A private home education is really a liberty issue, and it's very tough to see how a government operated home school could be in the best interests of liberty for home education," Smith said.

Because virtual charters are still under the curriculum and testing requirements of traditional public schools, home-school parents lose the right to choose faith-based materials. "If [parents] want credit for this, if they want a diploma later or a transcript or anything like that, they have to teach over the curriculum that is approved," Smith said. "That doesn't prevent them, outside the time they're getting credit, to augment [teaching materials] with Christian curriculum, but if they want to be in compliance with the program, they have to use whatever the charter school provides by way of curriculum."

One example of a virtual charter school that has faced opposition from home educators is the Interior Distance Education of Alaska, a statewide program created in 1997 that claims to be specifically tailored to the needs of home-school families. The program provides a per-student allotment of up to $2,000 annually for expenses such as textbooks, school supplies, and field trips.

A similar program, the Idaho Distance Education Academy [I-DEA], explicitly prohibits curriculum funds from being used to purchase "faith-based or doctrinal materials." Of concern to homeschoolers who value flexibility, the program establishes a mandatory attendance policy, with middle and high school students required to participate in "school" for a minimum of 990 hours per year. In addition, parents are required to electrically log in and report any student absences.

The Idaho Coalition of Home Educators [ICHE] has raised concerns about the I-DEA program, pointing out that public school districts have an incentive to recruit students since they receive government funds for each student enrolled in the online classes. School districts can use the extra dollars to supplement funds from traditionally enrolled public school students, according to ICHE. The home-school organization also claims that I-DEA allows public schools to receive credit for the achievements of homeschoolers.

A Trojan Horse

Smith said that money is "probably the primary reason" that virtual charters are targeting homeschoolers. "The difference between what it actually costs them to administer the program and what they get from the state goes directly to [the virtual charter]," Smith said. He said that, in some cases, public schools might be trying to influence what children are taught by using virtual charters as a kind of Trojan horse.

"There have been efforts to take the regulation of those who are under the virtual charter schools who are teaching their children at home and apply it to all of the homeschoolers," Smith said. "It looks like a good way to regulate home schooling, and that is the problem with these programs long term. They may look good now, but I have no doubt that the government, somewhere down the road, will try to tighten up on all of the homeschoolers."

Periodical and Internet Sources Bibliography

The following articles have been selected to supplement the diverse views presented in this chapter.

Bruno Behrend	"Research & Commentary: Digital Learning," The Heartland Institute, April 14, 2011. http://heartland.org.
Erin Dillon and Bill Tucker	"Lessons for Online Learning," *Education Next*, Spring 2011.
Trip Gabriel	"More Pupils Are Learning Online, Fueling Debate on Quality," *New York Times*, April 5, 2011.
LehighValleyLive.com	"Don't Cripple Pennsylvania's Cyber Charter Schools with Over-Regulation," March 14, 2010. www.lehighvalleylive.com.
Dan Lips	"Maryland Should Make the Most of Online Education," *Baltimore Sun*, September 27, 2010.
Katherine Mangu-Ward	"Traditional Schools Aren't Working. Let's Move Learning Online," *Washington Post*, March 28, 2010.
Jay Mathews	"Technology May Help Poor Schools by Starting with Rich Ones," *Washington Post*, May 28, 2010.
Jay Mathews	"Va. Is for Virtual, Not Charter, Schools," *Washington Post*, February 12, 2010.
Dave Murray	"Should Cyber Charter Get the Same Per-Student State Aid as Traditional Schools?," *Grand Rapids Press*, June 8, 2010.
Kristina Ribali	"A Mother's Plea for School Choice," Cascade Policy Institute, November 30, 2010. http://cascadepolicy.org.

OPPOSING
VIEWPOINTS®
SERIES

CHAPTER 4

How Can Charter Schools Be Improved?

Chapter Preface

In 2009 a progressive think tank, Minnesota 2020, released a report on the state's charter schools. The study, "Checking in on Charter Schools: An Examination of Charter School Finances," found that a majority of Minnesota charter schools do not follow basic financial guidelines and identified financial irregularities in 121 of the state's 145 charter schools. In its conclusion, the report stated that "charter school directors cannot handle simple financial accounting practices, nor do many charter schools have an interest in allowing the public to be aware of their machinations."

A 2010 investigation of Philadelphia charter schools by the city controller also turned up proof of mismanagement. A review of thirteen charter schools in Philadelphia revealed financial mismanagement and questionable practices at all thirteen schools. The city controller's final report found numerous missing documents, including proof of insurance and charter agreements; sketchy leasing agreements with questionable organizations; unethical or clearly corrupt construction, maintenance, and/or management contracts; inflated contracts and salaries; and numerous cases of ethical and legal violations, including conflicts of interest. "The charter school experiment is providing parents with educational choice and opportunities for their children outside of the normal public school route," said Alan Butkovitz, city controller of Philadelphia, about the scandal. "We must ensure that $300 million a year in taxpayers' money that goes to charter school education is being spent effectively and efficiently with appropriate controls and oversight to prevent and detect fraud, waste and abuse."

The examples of Minnesota and Philadelphia provide troubling evidence of mismanagement of the charter school system. Unfortunately, such examples are not uncommon. Corruption, fraud, and negligence have been major problems in charter schools across the country. Corruption and fraud are criminal problems perpetrated by unethical operators; but financial mismanagement or teaching and administrative incompetence can often be traced directly to poor training or a lack of experience with education management.

Studies have shown that charter school leaders have less experience with school leadership than the principals of traditional public schools. Almost 30 percent of charter school leaders have led a school for two years or less, compared with only 16 percent of traditional public school principals. Turnover is a key factor, as 71 percent of charter school leaders expect to have moved on to other positions within five years. In charter schools, administrators do not have the advantage of a district office to take care of school maintenance or financial management. Critics point out that many charter school leaders do not have a sufficient background in accounting and financial administration to handle the varied and demanding financial and administrative duties required in charter schools.

The experience and training of charter school leaders is one of the topics discussed in this chapter, which focuses on the ways in which charter schools can be improved. Additional topics include the racial segregation of charter schools, the role of competition, and the number of charter schools that should be allowed to open.

> "[In] the short term, opening fewer but stronger charter schools would be the best way to convince policy makers and the public of the potential of charter schools to help improve public schooling."

Fewer and Better Charter Schools Should Be Opened

Thomas Toch

Thomas Toch is the executive director of the Association of Independent Schools of Greater Washington. In the following viewpoint, he asserts that although the record of achievement for charter schooling has been mixed, the basic idea is still sound: Charter schools are a great fit for many communities and students and can be a catalyst of competition and reform for traditional public schools. Toch suggests that in the short term, there should be fewer and better charter schools opened, and that in the long run, more autonomy should be introduced into traditional school systems. This approach, he contends, will not only strengthen charter school performance, but also boost public school performance and community satisfaction with the US public school system at large.

Thomas Toch, "Reflections on the Charter School Movement," *Phi Delta Kappan*, May 2010. Reproduced by permission.

As you read, consider the following questions:

1. According to the author, how many charter schools are there in the United States?

2. How many students does Toch say are enrolled in charter schools?

3. Why does Toch state that it is difficult to expand charter schooling outside of major urban centers?

Two decades ago, I learned about charter schools while strolling through a Minneapolis suburb with Ted Kolderie, a civic gadfly who was helping local legislators craft a bill that would make Minnesota the first state to permit the hybrid public schools. He wanted to combat the bureaucracy of traditional public school systems, he told me, and to encourage educators to become entrepreneurs. Today, about 4,600 charter schools spread across 39 states and the District of Columbia, educating about 1.5 million students. They've become a permanent part of the education landscape. And now the [Barack] Obama administration is making charters a cornerstone of its multibillion-dollar federal education reform agenda. I've visited maybe 100 charter schools since my walk with Kolderie. Here's some of what I've learned.

Lessons of the Charter School Movement

Charter schools have brought many talented people to the cause of public school improvement. This new generation of social entrepreneurs includes Ivy League graduates and Rhodes Scholars committed to helping the disadvantaged and drawn to public schooling by the independence offered by charter schools.

The charter movement has also attracted bad actors more interested in enriching themselves than students. There are stories of educational failure and financial malfeasance in charter schools just as unscrupulous trade schools fed off the federal financial aid system for many years.

Some contend that the nearly 500 charter school closures between 2004–05 and 2008–09 (about 2,000 charters opened during the same period) are a sign of an effective market-place, one that rewards winners and punishes losers to a much greater degree than traditional public school systems. But, given the demand in urban centers for alternatives to traditional public schools, the closure of 500 charter schools (which, of course, is a good thing) reflects as much as anything a lack of scrutiny of charter school applications. For much of the past two decades, quantity has been a higher priority than quality in the charter school movement.

The Problem of Accountability

Only recently has the charter community begun to make good on its original pledge of more accountability in return for more autonomy, thanks to the work of people like Greg Richmond, president of the National Association of Charter School Authorizers, who have argued, correctly, that a few bad charter schools are likely to have a much greater influence on the prospects of the charter movement than a lot of good charters. But accountability remains weak in a number of key states, and the charter world remains deeply divided over whether the locus of accountability should rest with consumers or regulators.

Charter schools collectively have hardly been the salvation that many reformers had hoped. Researchers continue to debate the right traditional public school comparison groups. But it's clear there are at least as many bad charters as good ones and that, while a relative handful have produced truly outstanding results, many aren't any better than traditional public schools, and some are worse.

Charter Management Organizations

With over a half billion dollars in foundation funding and the financial expertise of venture-capital-like enterprises such as the San Francisco-based NewSchools Venture Fund, some four dozen nonprofit charter management organizations (CMOs) have set out to build networks of top charter schools. A decade into the experiment, they've managed to open about 350 schools with some 100,000 seats, a far cry from the 5,000 failing public schools that Secretary of Education Arne Duncan hopes to fix or replace. And many of the organizations are struggling financially and academically.

It would be much less difficult for CMOs to open more high-quality and financially sound schools if they received as much public funding as traditional public schools and didn't have to find and pay for their facilities. And it would be easier for them to make their budgets work if they weren't trying to expand.

The High Costs of Smaller Schools

But the high cost of the typically small schools (they average 300 students), intensive support for schools and students, and other features that have produced the best results have left a number of the organizations financially strapped. The 17 CMOs supported by the NewSchools Venture Fund reported spending an average of 18% of their revenue on their central offices in 2007–08 to make sure their schools got the help they needed to be successful—three times the level of central office spending allowed under the business plans of several of the organizations.

Attracting the talented teachers and principals willing to work the long hours needed to launch new schools in difficult environments has also proven challenging. The 17 CMOs in the NewSchools orbit reported that, in 2007–08, an average of 40% of their teachers had been in teaching two years or less. It's been hard to expand charter schooling outside major ur-

Establishing a Quality Standard

A key challenge that has limited the charter movement's success to date is the broad misalignment in expectations among charter operators, authorizers, funders, and other stakeholders about how to measure and judge school quality. Indeed, many believe that the vast diversity in charter school missions, educational models, and student populations, as well as differences in state accountability requirements and individual authorizer expectations, makes it impossible to establish common standards and measures of quality that are applicable and meaningful to all kinds of charter schools. The charter sector today has no basic, universal measures of school quality other than those shared with other public schools under the No Child Left Behind Act. It is no wonder that judgments about the performance of charter schools are so frequently ill-informed.

Of course, this weakness in performance evaluation is not confined to charter schools; it afflicts public education as a whole, greatly hobbling and constraining efforts to improve schools. Too often, current approaches to evaluating school performance rely on data that are seriously limited and misleading, unhelpful to schools, and inappropriate for high-stakes judgments. To fulfill the promise of the charter school movement and maximize its success and impact, the charter sector nationwide needs to clarify and commit to a common set of basic quality expectations and performance measures to define and assess charter school success.

"A Framework for Academic Quality," National Consensus Panel on Charter School Academic Quality, June 2008.

ban centers where entrepreneurial young educators want to live and where foundation funding is concentrated. The [National] Charter School Research Project reports that 41% of California's charters are in Los Angeles and 90% of Illinois's charters are in Chicago.

For-Profit Charters

The for-profit wing of the charter school movement hasn't fared significantly better in trying to achieve the reform trifecta of scale, quality, and sustainability. Touted two decades ago as an engine of revolutionary reform, in 2008–09 for-profit management companies that ran more than three schools ran 650 traditional public schools and charter schools enrolling 301,000 out of the nation's 55 million students, the Education [and the] Public Interest Center at the University of Colorado at Boulder reports. Two of the companies—K12 [Inc.] and Connections Academy—educated 50,000 of those students over the Internet.

Charters haven't influenced traditional public schools as much as school reformers had hoped. A few charter schools have demonstrated that disadvantaged students can be taught to sharply higher standards. But charters haven't produced enough competitive pressure on traditional public schools to cause them to embrace ambitious reforms the way the rise of FedEx led the U.S. Postal Service to launch Express Mail and other innovations. In many cities, charter schools have put more competitive pressure on urban Catholic schools than on public school systems, as significant numbers of parochial-school families migrate to tuition-free charter schools.

Keeping the Faith

Some charter advocates have lost faith in the reform strategy. Much has been made of historian Diane Ravitch's break with charters and other market-based reforms in her new book *The Death and Life of the Great American School System: How Test-*

ing and Choice Are Undermining Education. But no less significant is the conclusion by prominent conservative policy analyst Chester Finn that "charter schools are uneven at best."

Still, the original insight shared by Kolderie and other originators of the charter school concept is sound: The entrepreneurial ethic created by the independence that charter schools have over staffing, budgets, and instruction can be a powerful catalyst of school improvement. Successful schools as different as Deborah Meier's Central Park East secondary school and those in the KIPP [Knowledge Is Power Program] network have demonstrated the potential of such independence. We can't build the high-performing education system our economy demands on the bureaucratic foundations of traditional public schooling.

Smart and Effective Reforms

But the many troubles in the charter school movement also suggest that we cannot leave charter school quality to the market. Libertarian-leaning charter school advocates are wrong when they say that parents voting with their feet are sufficient to ensure that charter schools do right by students and taxpayers. And it's not enough to argue, as some advocates do, that charter schools need only be as good as the public schools they replace. How does that help students?

In the long run, the goal should be to introduce into traditional school systems the autonomy that charter schools enjoy today, a step that New York City is taking. But in the short term, opening fewer but stronger charter schools would be the best way to convince policy makers and the public of the potential of charter schools to help improve public schooling. Secretary of Education Arne Duncan has pressed states during the evolution of the federal Race to the Top school reform competition to lift caps on the number of new charter schools they permit. Perhaps, given the charter school movement's performance over the years, that shouldn't be his highest priority.

> "[The] expansion of charters in New York City brings us a little closer to realizing what only recently seemed an impossible dream: a good education for all children that doesn't depend on the luck of the draw."

More Charters Should Be Opened

Marcus A. Winters

Marcus A. Winters is a senior fellow at the Manhattan Institute. In the following viewpoint, he points out that in some urban areas, like New York City, admission to a charter school is determined by lottery, which he deems a random and unfair way to decide a child's future. In New York City, Winters maintains, charter schools are well run and a preferable option to traditional public schools in many areas. Winters argues that it is in the best interest of students in areas of underperforming traditional public schools to facilitate the opening of more high-performing charter schools, despite the opposition of critics and teachers' unions.

As you read, consider the following questions:

1. How many applicants were there for admission to Democracy Prep in Harlem in 2010?

2. According to Winters, how many charter schools are there in New York City?

3. Why does Winters assert that New York City's charter schools perform so well?

"Please, please, please," whispered the boy sitting to my left in the crowded auditorium, clenching his fists. Clearly too young for the sixth grade, he seemed to be praying for his brother, who sat nearby. If the brother's name was called from the podium, he would begin sixth grade next year at Democracy Prep, a four-year-old Harlem charter school. The odds were against it: A few days earlier, the 205 names being announced had been randomly drawn from a pool of 1,250 applicants. But finally it happened. "Yes!" the boys' mother yelped, smothering Democracy Prep's newest student in a bear hug. The younger brother beamed.

The Charter School Lottery

Still, most people's prayers weren't answered that day. Once the final name was called, disappointment weighed heavily on the faces of the unlucky. Nothing less was at stake than the future of 1,250 children. Democracy Prep's was the last of the charter-school lotteries for the entering class of 2010, which will be known within the school as the "College Class of 2021." Most students whose names weren't called will enter one of Harlem's dreadful traditional public schools, from which they're as likely to drop out as graduate.

So for children whose parents can't afford to pay private-school tuition or move to neighborhoods with good public schools, a simple roll of the dice determines whether or not they will get a quality education. That is horribly unfair to the losers. But the lotteries are proving how good New York City's charter schools are—and helping fuel the charters' growth in Gotham.

Charter Schools in New York City

Charter schools are taxpayer-funded public schools that operate free from many of the bureaucratic restrictions imposed by state and district policies and by collective-bargaining agreements with teachers. New York City has nearly 100 charter schools in all five boroughs, but most cluster into a few neighborhoods. Charters enroll about 15 percent of Harlem students, for instance, even though they serve less than 3 percent of children citywide.

The lotteries are necessary because demand for charter-school seats far exceeds supply. By law, enrollment is determined randomly—with students who live in the local school district getting preference—whenever a charter school receives more applicants than it has available seats. That was the case for all but one of the city's charter schools last year [in 2009].

The lottery mechanism varies by school. The Harlem Village Academies blindly pick index cards with children's names and contact information out of a box. Democracy Prep and the Harlem Success Academies use a computerized random-number generator. An independent auditor oversees each school's lottery, and statistical tests in past years have confirmed that these are indeed random draws. Most schools now conduct their lotteries privately, either because they want to avoid the media attention or because they can't stand seeing the pain on the faces of kids whose names aren't called. (Newark mayor Cory Booker, a charter-school supporter, is so greatly affected by the lotteries that he refuses to attend any more of them.)

Democracy Prep, however, continues to hold a public lottery, intent on showing the world thousands of flesh-and-blood parents desperate to get their children into better schools. My conservative estimate is that more than one-third of all fifth graders enrolled in public schools in Harlem's District 5 entered Democracy Prep's lottery this year.

The Promise of Democracy Prep

What motivates Harlem's parents and children to apply in such numbers to Democracy Prep is a chance to trade up from one of the city's lousiest middle schools to one of its best. Many of the students in Democracy Prep's lottery are zoned for a traditional public middle school called the Academy of Collaborative Education (ACE). According to the metric that New York City uses to evaluate its schools—a complicated mixture of student test scores and school environment—ACE is the city's single worst middle school.

Given a choice, no sane person would send a child to ACE. In the New York City Department of Education's annual survey last year, when asked to evaluate the statement "I feel safe in my school," 79 percent of ACE's teachers "strongly disagreed," while the remaining 21 percent just plain disagreed. The teachers were right to worry: ACE had qualified as a "persistently dangerous" school, according to the standards that New York State has established under the No Child Left Behind Act. To achieve that designation, a school must experience at least six "serious" incidents per 100 students for two consecutive years. Serious incidents include such offenses as homicide, robbery, assault resulting in serious physical injury, and use of a weapon.

Many believe that schools like ACE have such toxic environments because the students who attend them are monsters created by poverty and racism. But if that were true, you might expect Democracy Prep to be equally dangerous: its main campus sits directly across the street from ACE; the lottery's preference for children in the local district ensures that most students in the two schools are neighbors; and Seth Andrew, Democracy Prep's founder, estimates that about half of ACE's current students entered his school's lottery in past years. Nevertheless, in the city's survey, *all* of Democracy Prep's teachers agreed that they felt safe in school.

The Success of Democracy Prep

According to the city's metric, moreover, Democracy Prep is the highest-performing school in Harlem and among the 20 highest-performing middle schools in the entire city. And a commercial test that the school recently administered showed that its average student entered sixth grade reading at about the fifth-grade level and finished the year at nearly the eighth-grade level.

Democracy Prep doesn't boast a special curriculum, fancy classroom-management techniques, or smaller-than-average class sizes. Its success—like that of many good charter schools—has three primary ingredients: efficient use of funds, a culture of high expectations, and a "no excuses" approach to school discipline.

Efficient Money Management

Democracy Prep, like other city charters, spends about as much per pupil as the surrounding district public schools do: Though it doesn't receive capital funds from the state, it makes up the difference in philanthropic contributions and by locating the sixth grade in a public school virtually rent-free. But the school's charter status allows it to use its resources more wisely than the district schools do. Democracy Prep saves money by employing many young teachers, substituting 401(k)-style [retirement] plans for the gold-plated, defined-benefit pensions bestowed in the traditional public sector, and eliminating administrative bloat. Thanks to these savings, the school can pay its teachers 10 percent above the traditional public school pay scale. The school also has money left over to provide students with enriching activities: Before they graduate, Democracy Prep's kids, many of whom had rarely ventured out of their neighborhood, will have visited more than 75 college campuses and set foot on five continents. Again, all of this is done for about the same amount of money that advocates for traditional public schools say is insufficient to purchase even basic resources.

A Culture of Excellence

The second key to the school's success is its culture of excellence. As its name suggests, Democracy Prep teaches students that it's their responsibility to be active, engaged, and educated citizens. The school's motto stresses this message: "Work Hard. Go to College. Change the World!" At Democracy Prep, every adult is dedicated to sending every child to college—an attitude few would claim is widespread in the city's traditional public schools in poor neighborhoods. Teachers who don't believe that goal is reachable or are unwilling to do what's necessary to achieve it don't get hired, and those who manage to slip through the cracks don't last long. The college expectation permeates the atmosphere: Homerooms are named after universities, usually the teacher's alma mater, and college banners from across the nation adorn the hallways. Since the school's first cohort hasn't reached graduation yet, we can't know for sure how many of these children will graduate and go to college. But their test scores and the look in their eyes suggest that their prospects are far more promising than those of their peers at ACE.

The teachers live the culture of high expectations and accountability just as much as the students do. A principal in a typical public school observes his teachers in action once or twice a year, but administrators at Democracy Prep pop their heads into classrooms every day. And great teachers often jump at the chance to work in a school that pushes excellence. Last year, 4,000 teachers applied for about 20 openings at Democracy Prep.

The Popularity of Charter Schools

Charter schools are new, innovative public schools that are accountable for student results. They are designed to deliver programs tailored to educational excellence and the needs of the communities they serve.

Charter schools are one of the fastest and most successful growing reforms in the country. The first charter school opened its doors in St. Paul, Minnesota, in 1992 and now, almost two decades later, more than 5,000 charter schools are serving over 1.5 million children across 39 states and the District of Columbia.

Based on the belief that America's public schools should meet standards of excellence and be held accountable, parents are lining up to choose these innovative public schools that are able to meet the individual needs of their children.

"Ed Reform FAQs,"
Center for Education Reform, November 1, 2009.

Discipline Is Key

Discipline is the final and perhaps most important element of the school's success. Democracy Prep is one of several exceptional charter schools that apply the "no excuses" model pioneered by the Knowledge Is Power Program [KIPP], which now operates 82 charter schools in 19 states, including two in New York City. At Democracy Prep, kids sit at their desks and are expected to work at all times. They walk from one classroom to another quickly, quietly, and under adult supervision. The disciplinary policy is based on the Broken Windows approach that has worked wonders in big-city policing: The school deals with small infractions seriously and creates an environment in which major violations are simply unthinkable. On the day I visited Democracy Prep, the school took the uncommon step of requiring the sixth graders to eat lunch in absolute silence because they had been "mean" to one another recently. I felt no need to ask whether weapons had been involved in the meanness. During lunch at ACE, by contrast, kids scream, basketballs bounce, and young boys run around unchecked. Children seem happier in Democracy Prep's safe, structured environment, too. When you stroll through the school's hallways, you can feel curiosity, security, and even joy—a far cry from the noise and aggression that characterize ACE.

Criticisms of Charter Schooling

When critics of charter schools see places like Democracy Prep, they tend to respond with two arguments. The first is that Democracy Prep isn't typical. A few charter schools may be stellar, the critics admit, but most don't help children any more than traditional schools do.

In New York City, at least, that argument doesn't hold water. A recent study by Stanford University economist Caroline Hoxby found that about 45 percent of Gotham's charter-school students attend charters that have a positive influence on English proficiency, relative to the public schools that their students would have attended otherwise, of between 0.1 and 0.2 standard deviations (read "large difference"); for 31 percent of the students, it's more than 0.2 standard deviations (read "enormous difference"). Meanwhile, 16 percent attend charters that are roughly on par with their previous public schools, and only 8 percent attend charters that are worse. Hoxby's results in math were only slightly less positive.

The critics—led by the local teachers' union, the United Federation of Teachers (UFT)—focus on the few charters that are seriously underperforming, demanding that the city shut them down. That may indeed be the right approach with those schools, but the teachers' union is endorsing a glaring double standard, it's worth pointing out. When the city recently tried to close ACE and 18 other failing public schools, the UFT filed a lawsuit to keep them open, raising procedural objections to the closures. If a state Supreme Court judge hadn't ruled in the UFT's favor, last year's entering class of sixth graders would have been the last to endure the mayhem within ACE's walls.

Quality of Students

The critics' second argument is that charters' impressive performance is a mirage. The reason that New York charter schools report better educational outcomes than traditional public schools, they say, is that the charters attract students with higher proficiency levels. The critics claim that charters are really no more effective than the traditional schools; they're just starting with better students.

Ironically, what allows charter-school advocates to rebut that argument is the very lotteries that will one day, they hope, be unnecessary. The charters' random-selection policy has allowed Hoxby's team to evaluate them with a randomized field trial (RFT), the kind of experiment often described by social scientists as the "gold standard" in research design. RFTs resemble the clinical trials performed by pharmaceutical companies, which test a new drug by assembling a pool of subjects, randomly assigning subjects to receive either the drug or a placebo, and then comparing the subjects' condition. Similarly, Hoxby took a pool of subjects (students applying to New York City charter schools); took advantage of the random nature of the lotteries, which assigned the subjects either to charters or to traditional public schools; and then compared their academic achievement. Because access to a charter school is the only meaningful difference between the two groups—both applied to charter schools, after all—

comparing the groups' later achievement really will tell us what effect charters have on student performance.

The RFT yielded unambiguously positive results. For the average applicant, the study's authors showed, winning a spot in a charter school in kindergarten leads to academic gains that close most of the test-score gap between the average student in Harlem and the average student in *Scarsdale*—a wealthy New York City suburb known for its high-performing schools—by the end of eighth grade. The charter-school critics have offered scant rebuttal to this remarkable finding, preferring to cite a study by another Stanford professor, Margaret Raymond, which found wide variation in charter-school performance nationwide. But when Raymond studied New York City's charter schools, she found results similar to Hoxby's. Many think that the reason that New York does better than the rest of the country is the state's tough charter-authorization process.

Recent Movies on Charter-School Lotteries

It turns out that charter-school lotteries aren't merely useful statistical tools; they also make for gripping theater, as two new documentaries demonstrate. In *The Lottery*, which opened at the Tribeca Film Festival this spring, first-time filmmaker Madeleine Sackler follows four kids hoping to be selected in the Harlem Success Academies' lottery. And *Waiting for "Superman,"* in theaters this fall, offers the best evidence to date that charter schools are no longer a reform sought by conservatives alone: The film was directed by Davis Guggenheim of *An Inconvenient Truth* fame, and it will be distributed and publicized by a major studio, Paramount. The climax of both films arrives when students learn their fate at the charter-school lotteries. They're suspenseful moments: Viewers know that these are real children, some of whom may not get another chance for success in life.

Luckily, charters are expanding rapidly in New York. This spring—after a heated, yearlong battle in which the Hoxby study was repeatedly cited—the New York State Legislature raised the cap on the state's allowed number of charters from 200 to 460. With another 114 charter schools expected to open in New York City in the next four to five years [2010–2015] and current schools continuing to expand, charters could soon serve as many as 10 percent of Gotham's kids and the lion's share of students in low-income neighborhoods like Harlem and the South Bronx.

Random chance shouldn't determine whether Harlem children go to great schools or broken ones. But thanks to random chance, we can say that the benefits accruing to New York students from charter schools are no longer in dispute. And the expansion of charters in New York City brings us a little closer to realizing what only recently seemed an impossible dream: a good education for all children that doesn't depend on the luck of the draw.

> "Charter schools that can elevate diversity and meet the educational standards should be rewarded with government dollars; those that violate civil rights provisions should not; in fact, they should be closed."

Charter Schools Are Racially Segregated

Noah Lederman

Noah Lederman is an author and a journalist. In the following viewpoint, he maintains that there is a growing concern that the charter school movement is contributing to the problem of increasing segregation in public schools. Lederman argues that allowing segregation—racial, religious, or socioeconomic—in charter schools reduces opportunities for students and limits their exposure to diverse perspectives on society that will greatly benefit them in life. He states that federal funds should not be used to facilitate segregation and that charter schools need to make a stronger effort to promote diversity.

As you read, consider the following questions:

1. According to a January 2010 report by the Civil Rights Project, what percentage of Latino charter school students attend schools where 90 percent or more of the school's students are minorities?

2. What did the US Supreme Court decision on the *Brown v. Board of Education* case do, according to the author?

3. What programs does Lederman recommend to facilitate diversity in charter schools?

If you happen to walk through a New York City public school today, you'll find your melting pots in place—heterogeneous students boiled down into homogenous groups. Or, as multiculturalists put it, students of various ethnicities, races, and religions commingle in discernible salad bowls that allow for the celebration of diversity.

As a New York City teacher, I've noticed these pots or bowls present in the building; but I've also watched these metaphors lose meaning as some students find comfort isolated with peers of their race, religion, or ethnicity.

Charter Schools and the Problem of Segregation

Although the public schools must work to promote diversity, there is a greater concern when it comes to segregation in education. Since 1990, the growing charter school movement, which has tried to address the educational needs that public schools have failed to meet, is quickly contributing to segregation.

In a January 2010 report, the Civil Rights Project of UCLA [University of California, Los Angeles] contends that the charter school movement "has been a civil rights failure." According to the report, "charter schools enroll a disproportionate share of black students and expose them to the highest level of segregation. Almost a third end up in apartheid schools with zero to one percent white classmates, the very kind of schools that decades of civil rights struggles fought to abolish in the South." The authors also indicate that Latino students face "triple segregation" by race, class, and fluency. Additionally, half of the Latino charter school students attend schools where 90% or more of the school's students are minorities. Some states are also experiencing the "white flight" phenomenon, when white students head off to charter schools, leaving behind poorly funded public schools that begin to resemble American schools of the early '50s.

"[T]he rapid growth of charter schools has been expanding a sector that is even more segregated than the public schools," the authors conclude.

We Cannot Overlook Segregation

Segregation as a result of charter schools may have been overlooked in the belief that charter schools would offer a superior education, but in a 2009 report, the Center for Research [on] Education Outcomes at Stanford University claims that students in charter schools are not performing as well as students in traditional public schools.

Arne Duncan, the secretary of education, acknowledges that education is the civil rights issue of our time, yet charter schools receive increased federal funding to operate.

As Black History Month [February] draws to a close, there is a need to refocus our efforts on *Brown v. Board of Education [of Topeka]*, which ended legalized segregation in schools nearly fifty-six years ago. Although today's school segregation is mostly self-imposed, it is problematic when government funds allow these schools to operate and when Supreme Court decisions render *Brown* impotent, as in 2007, when the court ruled that school districts are not allowed to consider racial diversity as a factor for school assignments.

"School Choice Leaves Equality Behind," cartoon by Jesse Springer. www.CartoonStock.com.

The Consequences of Segregation

Allowing our schools to be segregated promotes a future of distrust and disunity. Separating youngsters along race, religious, or socioeconomic lines reduces the opportunity for social networking and limits the chance of exposure to diverse perspectives on society. Also, certain content will begin to lose relevances—How can you possibly teach [Martin Luther] King's Dream in a classroom devoid of black or white faces?

Promoting Diversity

Schools need to remain desegregated. To promote diversity, the pre- and post-school day will require more funding, namely transportation and after-school programs. Federally funded transport allows students from mostly homogenous neighborhoods to spread out and attend schools that match their interests and needs. After-school programs provide an environment for collaboration and community. But with recent and future budget cuts, these programs die first. For instance, New York City is considering ending free MetroCards for the thousands of students that ride the trains and buses to school. This will increase school segregation, by keeping local schools filled with the color and class of their neighborhood. If times are so hard for the city, can't partly subsidized Metro-Cards be offered?

Not all charter schools are failing, some are even quite successful, but those that are unintentionally fueling segregation are hindering a child's learning potential. Take English Language Learners [ELLs]. Charter schools may offer ELLs the opportunity for intense language instruction in segregated classrooms; but in a diversified school, ELLs will receive separate language instruction, as well as exposure to native speakers in an organic environment. Though charter schools are not promoting racial segregation, just as Dr. Kenneth Clark illustrated in the *Brown* case when he highlighted a black child's feeling of inferiority with the "Doll Test," [a psychological experiment using dolls that showed that black child had been inculcated with a sense of racial inferiority at a young age because of racial prejudice at the time] there is an implied inferiority that will continue to manifest in the minds of these young students learning in isolated environments.

No Public Funds for Segregation

This is not to say we should eliminate charter schools, but we should not allow federal funds to reinstitute segregation. Charter schools that can elevate diversity and meet the educational standards should be rewarded with government dollars; those that violate civil rights provisions should not; in fact, they should be closed.

In the past six decades, America has come a long way to eliminate school segregation and promote the beginnings of diversity. Though segregation as a result of charter schools is not of the same viciousness as Jim Crow [a series of laws that mandated racial segregation in all public facilities from 1876–

1965], it still has the potential to lead us in the wrong direction. Ignoring integration is what established the climates of Jerusalem and Johannesburg, Belfast and Baghdad, and the United States of America in the century after slavery. If charter schools continue to unintentionally foster segregation and the federal government helps to fund this disservice, passing up the opportunity to provide guidance and offer reform, expect our metaphorical melting pot or mixed salad bowl to look more like the isolated layers of a seven layer dip or the sectioned off segments of a vegetable platter.

> "[The] racial patterns we observe in charter schools are the result of the choices students and families make as they seek more attractive schooling options."

The Charges of Racial Segregation in Charter Schools Are Overstated

Gary Ritter, Nathan Jensen, Brian Kisida, and Joshua McGee

Gary Ritter is professor of education policy at the University of Arkansas. Nathan Jensen, Brian Kisida, and Joshua McGee are research associates in the Department of Education Reform at the University of Arkansas. In the following viewpoint, they take issue with a January 2010 study from the Civil Rights Project (CRP) that concludes that segregation in charter schools is much more prevalent and pronounced than in traditional public schools. Ritter, Jensen, Kisida, and McGee argue that the data reveal small differences in the level of overall segregation between charter schools and traditional public schools. They point out that the CRP study fails to take into account that charter schools are usually located in areas with disadvantaged popula-

tions to help the students who most need it; therefore, charter schools tend to enroll higher percentages of minorities than will the average traditional public school.

As you read, consider the following questions:

1. How does the CRP report define "hypersegregated"?

2. According to the CRP report, what percentage of charter school students attend school in a city?

3. What percentage of American students attend traditional public schools, as indicated by the CRP report?

In January 2010, the UCLA [University of California, Los-Angeles]-based Civil Rights Project (CRP) released "Choice Without Equity: Charter School Segregation and the Need for Civil Rights Standards." The study intended to report on, among other things, levels of racial segregation in charter schools across the United States. The authors use 2007–08 data from the U.S. Department of Education's Common Core of Data (CCD) to compare the racial composition of charter schools to that of traditional public schools at three different levels of aggregation: nationwide; within 40 states and the District of Columbia; and within 39 metropolitan areas with large enrollments of charter school students. Based on these comparisons, the authors conclude, incorrectly in our view, that charter schools experience severe levels of racial segregation compared to traditional public schools (TPS).

The Problem of Segregation in Charter Schools

We will show that, when examined more appropriately, the data actually reveal small differences in the level of overall segregation between the charter school sector and the traditional public school sector. Indeed, we find the majority of students in the central cities of metropolitan areas, in both charter and traditional public schools, attend school in intensely segregated settings. Our findings are similar to those in a 2009 report by RAND, in which researchers focused on segregation in five large metropolitan areas (Chicago, Denver, Milwaukee, Philadelphia, and San Diego)—areas that were also included in the CRP report. The RAND authors, with the benefit of student-level data, follow students who move from traditional public schools into charter schools and conclude that these transfers have "surprisingly little effect on racial distributions across the sites." The authors of the RAND report write:

> Across 21 comparisons (seven sites with three racial groups each), we find only two cases in which the average difference between the sending TPS and the receiving charter school is greater than 10 percentage points in the concentration of the transferring student's race.

The RAND report, based on a superior methodology, provides strong evidence that the CRP claims are off base. Their findings, coupled with our own, offer a significantly different portrayal of segregation in charter schools than the CRP report. We find no basis for the allegations made by the CRP authors, who argue that charter school enrollment growth, based on the free choices of mostly minority families, represents a "civil rights failure."

While we find fault with the methodology employed by the CRP authors, and with their conclusions, we recognize that the questions addressed by the CRP, in this report and in scores of earlier ones, concern issues of importance for policy makers and the public alike. With the billions of dollars invested each year in public schools, both traditional and charter, and the millions of hours that we compel our children to attend these schools, it is critical that we have a basic understanding of the school environment that we are providing. Moreover, given the history of forced racial segregation in our nation's schools, we must be ever-attentive to these issues.

Indeed, because these questions are of such significance, it is imperative that they be addressed carefully and correctly.

The Wrong Approach

Unfortunately, the analyses employed in the CRP report do not meet this standard. The authors begin by presenting a great deal of descriptive data on the overall enrollment and aggregate racial composition in public charter schools compared to traditional public schools. Based only on enrollments aggregated to the national and state level, the authors repeatedly highlight the overrepresentation of black students in charter schools in an attempt to portray a harmful degree of segregation. But comparisons of simple averages at such a high level of aggregation can obscure wide differences in school-level demographics among both charter and traditional public schools. It is like having your feet in the oven and your head in the icebox, and saying that, on average, the temperature is just right.

After this descriptive overview, the authors address the question of racial segregation in a more appropriate way. In this analysis, the CRP authors define as "hypersegregated" any school with a 90 percent minority population or a 90 percent white population. Their aim is to determine if charter students nationwide are more or less likely to attend school in such hypersegregated environments. However, a critical flaw undermines this comparison and all of the analyses that follow. In every case, whether the authors examine the numbers at the national, state, or metropolitan level, they compare the racial composition of *all* charter schools to that of *all* traditional public schools. This comparison is likely to generate misleading conclusions for one simple reason, as the authors themselves point out on the first page of the executive summary and then again on page 57 of the full report: "the concentration of charter schools in urban areas skews the charter school enrollment towards having higher percentages of poor and minority students."

Location, Location, Location

In other words, the geographic placement of charter schools practically ensures that they will enroll higher percentages of minorities than will the average public school in the nation, in states, and in large metropolitan areas. Further, because serving disadvantaged populations is the stated mission of many charter schools, they seek out locations near disadvantaged populations intentionally. Instead of asking whether all students in charter schools are more likely to attend segregated schools than are all students in traditional public schools, we should be comparing the racial composition of charter schools to that of nearby traditional public schools. Employing this method, we could compare the levels of segregation for the students in charter schools to what they would have experienced had they remained in their residentially assigned public schools.

If we acknowledge this standard for valid comparisons, we can quickly dismiss the national and state-level comparisons, which constitute the bulk of the CRP report. According to the authors' own numbers ... , more than half (56 percent) of charter school students attend school in a city, compared to less than one-third (30 percent) of traditional public school students. Thus, any national comparisons are inappropriate, as these two groups of students are inherently dissimilar. The authors employ this same flawed strategy individually for each of the 40 states included in their analysis. Again, comparing the segregation in charter schools in a state, which are concentrated in heavily minority central cities, to that in traditional public schools throughout the state, reveals nothing about the reality of racial segregation in charter schools.

The examples that the authors draw from these state-level comparisons are almost humorous at times. For example, consider the following point from page 43 of the report:

> In some cases, like Idaho, charter school students across all races attend schools of white isolation: majorities of students of all races are in 90–100% white charter schools.

No kidding! The state of Idaho is nearly 95 percent white. Obviously, this is not a charter phenomenon, yet the authors brazenly use this as evidence for their claims without making any mention of the corresponding figure for the traditional public schools in the state.

Hypersegregation

Finally, the authors consider the hypersegregation in charter and traditional public schools individually within 39 metropolitan areas. But even within the large Census Bureau–defined Core Based Statistical Areas (CBSAs) [CBSAs are metro and micropolitan (more than 10,000 people but less than 50,000) areas of the country] used as proxies for metropolitan areas, charters are still disproportionately located in low-SES (socioeconomic status) urban areas, while traditional public schools are dispersed throughout the entire CBSA. For example, the authors note that in the Washington, D.C., CBSA, 91 percent of students in charter schools attend hypersegregated schools, while only 20 percent of students in that same area attend hypersegregated traditional public schools. A quick look at the geographical placement of charter schools in the D.C. metro area, however, shows why such a comparison is inappropriate. The D.C. metro CBSA contains 1,186 traditional public schools, 1,026 of which are in Virginia, Maryland, and even West Virginia; only 13 percent of the traditional public schools in the D.C. CBSA are actually situated in the racially isolated District of Columbia. On the other hand, 93 percent of the charter schools in the D.C. CBSA are located in D.C. In other words, nearly all of the area's charter schools are in D.C., while the vast majority of the traditional public schools the authors use in their comparisons are located in the largely suburban or exurban areas of surrounding states. For the 39 CBSAs examined by the authors, only 22 percent of the traditional public schools were located in central cities, compared to 51 percent of the charter schools.

A Tighter Comparison

It is indeed likely that, with the right analysis and the proper questions, the conclusion would not be as clear as portrayed by the CRP authors. We modified the CRP analysis by comparing the percentage of students in hypersegregated minority charters within the central city of each CBSA to the percentage of students in hypersegregated minority traditional public schools within the same central city. For example, for the Washington, D.C., CBSA, we included only schools located within the District of Columbia. The data we obtained for this comparison are publicly available from the Common Core of Data, so the CRP researchers could have conducted their analysis at this level. Of course, even this analysis is not perfect. Only following students at the individual level would reveal precisely what effect charters are having on segregation.

We focus our reanalysis on the data presented by the authors in their report. The focal measures in this table are shown in the last two columns, where the authors present the percentage of charter school students (from the entire metropolitan area) in schools with greater than 90 percent minority students alongside the similar figure for traditional public schools. The problematic figure in this table is the percentage of traditional public school students in hypersegregated schools used as the point of comparison which shows the bias entailed for the 8 largest metropolitan areas by the CRP report.

The Gap Narrows

Using our method rather than the CRP method, the share of charter students attending hypersegregated schools is shown to be much less divergent from the share of students attending traditional public schools.

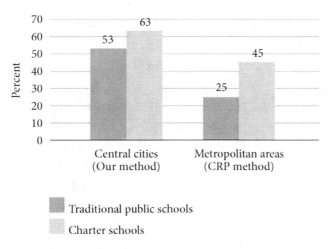

NOTE: Hypersegregated schools are those with student populations that are more than 90 percent non-white. Data are student-weighted.

SOURCE: Civil Rights Project, "Choice without Equity," and authors' calculations from the 2007–08 Common Core of Data

TAKEN FROM: Gary Ritter, Nathan Jensen, Brian Kisida, and Joshua McGee, "A Closer Look at Charter Schools and Segregation," *Education Next*, Summer 2010.

The Difference in Methods

Whether or not we believe that charter schools are more segregated than traditional public schools depends largely on which set of traditional public schools serve as a comparison. The data for these eight very large metropolitan areas, representing more than half of the enrollment for the entire data set, demonstrate how the CRP method overstates the relative levels of segregation in the charter sector. For example, under the CRP method, 91.2 percent of the charter students in the D.C. CBSA are in hypersegregated minority schools, as compared to just 20.9 percent of the students in traditional public schools. Using the central-city method, the percentage of students in hypersegregated minority charters stays roughly the same, but the percentage of students in hypersegregated minority traditional publics skyrockets to 85 percent.

In fact, in the vast majority of the 39 metro areas reviewed in the CRP report, the application of our central-city comparison decreases (relative to the flawed CRP analysis) the level of segregation in the charter sector as compared to the traditional public school sector. Importantly, unlike the CRP authors, we also compute and present the overall average results. Using the best available unit of comparison, we find that 63 percent of charter students in these central cities attend school in intensely segregated minority schools, as do 53 percent of traditional public school students. Thus, while it appears that charter students are, on average, more likely to attend hypersegregated minority schools, the difference between the charter and traditional public sector is far less stark than the CRP authors suggest.

The Right Question

Our analysis presents a more accurate, but still imperfect, picture of the levels of racial segregation in the charter sector relative to the traditional public-school sector. Ideally, to examine the issue of segregation, we would pose the question, Are the charter schools that students attend more or less segregated than the traditional public schools these students would otherwise attend? Unfortunately, our data linking schools to cities do not allow for this analysis.

Even within many of the central cities in the metropolitan areas listed above, there is a great deal of racial segregation. And most available data suggest that charter schools are popping up in areas where the students are poor and disadvantaged and need additional educational options. Public charter schools are simply less likely to open in economically advantaged, mostly white neighborhoods. Thus, even our analysis likely underestimates the true levels of racial segregation in the specific traditional public schools that charter students are leaving. Indeed, a more fine-grained analysis (similar to the study conducted by RAND) in which we compared the levels of segregation in public charter schools to that of the traditional public schools in the same neighborhood would be preferable. The RAND report is particularly relevant here because it focuses on student-level data from Chicago, Denver, Milwaukee, Philadelphia, and San Diego, five metropolitan areas highlighted in the CRP report. By examining student-level transfers, the authors are able to determine the extent to which students move into schools with higher concentrations of their own race and thereby increase the overall level of segregation. Using this strategy, the RAND researchers found,

> Transfers to charter schools did not create dramatic shifts in the sorting of students by race or ethnicity in any of the sites included in the study. In most sites, the racial composition of the charter schools entered by transferring students was similar to that of the TPSs from which the students came.

Our own similar analysis of student-level transfers to charters in the Little Rock, Arkansas, area over the past five years tells much the same story. While many of the students transferred into Little Rock charter schools that were racially segregated, these students generally left traditional public schools that were even more heavily segregated.

Acknowledging the Truth

The authors of the Civil Rights Project report conclude,

> Our new findings demonstrate that, while segregation for blacks among all public schools has been increasing for

nearly two decades, black students in charter schools are far more likely than their traditional public school counterparts to be educated in intensely segregated settings.

Our analysis suggests that these claims are certainly overstated. Furthermore, the authors fail to acknowledge two significant truths.

First, the majority of students in central cities, in both the public charter sector and in the traditional public sector, attend intensely segregated minority schools. Neither sector has cause to brag about racial diversity, but it seems clear that the CRP report points its lens in the wrong direction by focusing on the failings of charter schools. As the authors themselves note, across the country only 2.5 percent of public school children roam the halls in charter schools each day; the remaining 97.5 percent are *compelled* to attend traditional public schools. And we know that, more often than not, the students attending traditional public schools in cities are in intensely segregated schools. If we are truly concerned about limiting segregation, then this is where we should look to address the problem.

Second, and perhaps more important, the fact that poor and minority students flee segregated traditional public schools for similarly segregated charters does not imply that charter school policy is imposing segregation upon these students. Rather, the racial patterns we observe in charter schools are the result of the choices students and families make as they seek more attractive schooling options. To compare these active parental choices to the forced segregation of our nation's past (the authors of the report actually call some charter schools "apartheid" schools) trivializes the true oppression that was imposed on the grandparents and great-grandparents of many of the students seeking charter options today.

> "Education activists must realize inte-
> gration is often less of a concern to ur-
> ban families than the quality of educa-
> tion."

The Academic Achievement of Charter Schools Is More Important than Integration

RiShawn Biddle

RiShawn Biddle is an author and the editor of the Dropout Nation *blog. In the following viewpoint, he maintains that arguments that charter schools are too segregated ignore the reality
that most parents care more about the quality of their child's
education than other factors. Biddle suggests that much of the
criticism over segregation in charter schools comes from education activists who are against school choice and the growth of the
charter school movement. He recommends ending restrictions on
charter school expansion to end segregation in charter schools.*

As you read, consider the following questions:

1. According to a 2009 RAND study, how much more
   likely to attend college are charter school students than
   those attending traditional public schools in Chicago
   and Florida?

2. How does Biddle characterize President Barack Obama's attitude toward charter schools?

3. How does the author characterize the role that state laws establishing charters plays in segregation in the schools?

It's no longer surprising to see Al Sharpton [a political and civil rights activist] team up with New York City Schools Chancellor Joel Klein to cheer on the growth of the charter school movement. After all, it is one of the few innovations that have improved the quality of education for minority students in America's urban communities. Last month [December 2009], three charters with mostly minority enrollments— KIPP [Knowledge Is Power Program] Houston, Animo Leadership, and the Preuss School—landed on *U.S. News & World Report*'s annual list of best-performing high schools. A study released this past March [2009] by the RAND Corporation shows that children attending charters in Chicago and Florida are 7–15 percent more likely to attend college than those attending traditional public schools.

The Success of the Charter School Movement

This success, along with the movement's near-messianic zeal for improving the conditions of education for children, has won over parents looking to keep their kids out of the nation's dropout factories. There are now 38 urban school systems in which 10 percent or more of the students attend charters, according to the National Alliance for Public Charter Schools. In New Orleans, Washington, D.C., and Detroit, charters now account for more than half of school enrollment.

The Fly in the Ointment

But according to education activists such as Century Foundation senior fellow Richard Kahlenberg and Gary Orfield of the Civil Rights Project at UCLA [University of California, Los

Angeles], charters represent "racial isolation" and "minority segregation," and their presence "enforces unequal educational opportunities." Why? Because few white children, especially those from middle-class households, attend them.

This argument ignores the reality that quality of teaching, rigor of instruction, and economic status are far bigger factors in shaping a child's academic achievement than is the racial makeup of his school.

Unlike the Sharptons of the civil rights movement, these activists are more comfortable strolling along the manicured lawns of Harvard than standing on the gritty street corners of Cleveland. Charter schools have never been their cup of tea. What's set them on edge this time is Pres. Barack Obama, who has made charter school expansion the cornerstone of his school reform agenda. Through the $4.3 billion Race to the Top program, pronouncements from U.S. Secretary of Education Arne Duncan, and even his own bully pulpit, Obama is successfully coaxing states such as California to eliminate restrictions on the number of charter schools and to finance charters at the same levels that they finance traditional public schools.

Politically Motivated Opposition

Orfield, Kahlenberg, and other activists feel that Obama is betraying his campaign promises to focus on poverty and integration. They are particularly displeased with the administration's unwillingness to pour federal dollars into expanding magnet schools, even though magnets themselves have done little to foster integration or improve the academic performance of minority and poor students. So the activists—normally reflexively antagonistic toward anything the public education establishment holds dear—find themselves working hand in hand with school districts, teachers' unions, and other charter school opponents. At a conference held this past November at Howard University, civil rights groups such as the

NAACP Legal Defense [and Educational] Fund chided the administration for focusing less on integrating charters than on creating more of them.

At the heart of their opposition is the very concept of choice that underlies the existence of charters. They note that this can lead to self-segregation, which to them is as much an anathema as state-enforced Jim Crow [a series of laws that enforced the idea of "separate but equal," or segregation] discrimination. Minorities and the poor, according to this view, can't receive the same quality of education as their white middle-class peers unless they attend school *with* these peers. Declares Orfield: "Choice can be either a path toward real opportunity and equity or toward segregated and unequal education."

A Call for Quotas

Integration activists want state and federal officials to hold charters to the same levels of compliance with affirmative action laws as school districts under court-issued desegregation orders. In November, the Civil Rights Project released a report calling for federal education officials to essentially require charters to develop race- and ethnicity-based admissions quotas. That the report offers little evidence of charter school students' being ill-served by a lack of diversity didn't stop authors Erica Frankenberg and Genevieve Siegel-Hawley from proclaiming that this was "troubling."

But federal regulations can't compel integration; students tend to segregate themselves by race and class even within the most diverse schools. Three decades' worth of research reveals that segregation may not even be the most important cause of achievement gaps. The low quality of instruction provided by America's teaching corps—many members of which lack subject-knowledge competency—has an even greater impact on minority students and poor whites. As studies—such as a 2003 report by Dallas Independent School District researchers

Sitha Babu and Robert Mendro—point out, teaching quality may have a greater influence on student achievement than socioeconomic background. There's also the adverse impact of school district practices (many of which are shaped by union contracts and state laws), which often allow the most talented teachers to flee poor, mostly minority classrooms.

Charter Authorization Laws

Some activists also fail to realize that state laws establishing charters play a much larger role than self-selection in determining the homogeneousness of enrollments. Most states restrict the location of charters and, sometimes, even the type of students who can enroll. In Missouri, charters can only be opened in St. Louis and Kansas City, competing with school districts that have mostly black enrollment; Tennessee only allows charters to enroll students who previously attended other charters, were formerly enrolled in academically failing traditional public schools, or have failed the state's standardized tests.

Many states' requirement that charter school petitions be approved by traditional school districts—a rule that often exempts schools slated for urban locales—also deters diversity. Suburban school districts, in particular, have little reason to bring competing schools into their own backyards. There are fewer charters in Maryland and Virginia, which have this requirement, than in neighboring D.C., which doesn't—even though D.C. has a far smaller student population.

Focusing on Quality Education

Education activists must realize integration is often less of a concern to urban families than the quality of education. Many of them have experienced integration firsthand through forced busing efforts during the 1970s and 1980s. And, like Harvard professor (and onetime integration advocate) Charles Ogletree, these parents realize that integration was little more than a "false promise," and they also feel that integration denied them chances to interact with successful role models who looked like them. Minority parents are also dismayed by the tendency of school district bureaucracies to regard them as nuisances and bystanders. Charters, with their demand for more parental engagement, are much more appealing.

If we end restrictions on charter school expansion, then choice, integration, and academic quality can all become a reality. As Chicago mayor Richard Daley and his former colleague in Indianapolis, Bart Peterson, figured out, offering more charters may even lure white middle-class families from suburbs; allowing the growth of charters in suburbia may also foster diversity. But charter schools won't solve all these problems. It is also critical to improve the quality of teaching and reform ineffective school district hiring practices.

These steps are more likely to stem achievement gaps and achieve true racial equality than the outmoded prescriptions that activists are still peddling.

> *"To get schools to respond more mean-*
> *ingfully to competitive pressure, incen-*
> *tives and rules must be changed in or-*
> *der to ensure that the competitive*
> *pressure is actually felt."*

Market-Driven Competition Enhances Both Public and Charter Schools

Frederick M. Hess

Frederick M. Hess is an author and the director of educational policy studies at the American Enterprise Institute. In the follow-ing viewpoint, he argues that charter schools can provide the market-driven competition needed to motivate the necessary re-forms of traditional public schools if government does not over-regulate the system or subsidize failing institutions. Hess finds that proponents of school choice are not willing to do the hard work to fight for a friendlier playing field for charter schools, leaving the movement at a distinct disadvantage. He outlines a number of steps to improve the practical and political prospects of market-oriented school choice reform.

As you read, consider the following questions:

1. According to the author, how much do charter schools get for every dollar that school districts receive?

2. According to the annual poll in *Education Next*, how much has popular support for vouchers declined between 2007 and 2010?

3. What does the author perceive as a real opportunity for third parties when it comes to providing information on school performance?

A key feature of genuine markets is, of course, competition. In evaluating whether choice "works," what matters is not only whether escape routes to private or charter schools offer some students better educational alternatives, but also whether school-choice programs make traditional district schools better.

The Competition Question

Any observer who takes market theory seriously would probably respond, "Of course they do." But because of the peculiarities of American education, the answer is hardly so obvious. After all, market dynamics depend upon consumer behavior, regulatory frameworks, labor-market considerations, and incentives and consequences for producers and consumers. Competition matters only when it pinches, and the reality is that competition in K–12 education has not yet been given a robust test.

Still, there is some evidence that districts and schools may respond to even the mild competitive pressures that choice currently exerts. In 2003, Jay Greene examined Florida's A+ voucher program and reported that those low-performing schools that risked having their students granted vouchers to attend private alternatives were improving "in direct proportion to the challenge they face[d] from voucher competition."

In 2005, scholars Paul Peterson and Martin West reported similar findings. Under the accountability standards imposed by Florida in 2002, students at public schools that received "F" performance grades became subject to the threat of vouchers if they continued to perform poorly; Peterson and West concluded that students at schools put under the gun "performed at a higher level in the subsequent year than did students at similar schools not so threatened."

More recent research confirms the same patterns. After the Florida Supreme Court ruled in 2006 that the portion of the A+ program that funded private-school vouchers was unconstitutional, the state created an alternative program (which relies on private funding incentivized by tax credits to corporations). In June of this year [2010], economist David Figlio released a study of the new voucher program reporting that students in Florida public schools with a diverse array of private schools in close proximity showed slightly larger achievement gains than students in public schools with fewer nearby alternatives. Figlio also determined that student gains were larger in those schools at risk of losing state funds tied to the proportion of low-income students they enroll. Figlio concluded that the public schools' response to competition was real, although limited: "What we find is certainly positive and statistically strong," he explained, "but it's not like public schools are revolutionizing overnight because of this."

Misinterpreting Results

One challenge in interpreting these results is gauging whether the market-induced improvements reflect attempts to fundamentally rethink or re-engineer a school or district, or merely a re-allocation of effort and resources from untested activities to tested ones. This matters a lot, because quick-fix measures—like, say, shifting time from science or art to reading instruction—may improve student test performance (and thus answer a competitive threat) without signifying any attempt to boost productivity or overhaul cost structures, staffing, operations, or management. Moreover, in most cases, district responses to choice-induced competition have primarily been changes in marketing and outreach—such as the distribution of t-shirts and ads on local billboards intended to persuade parents to keep their children in their local public schools. Choice advocates have historically erred in reading these developments as signs of bigger changes to come.

It has been a mistake, in other words, to expect public schools to behave like the private sector—where competition, investor demand, and personal consequences for success or failure drive executives to press on productivity and the bottom line, and where executives have substantial leeway to remove, reward, and otherwise recognize employees based on their contributions to organizational improvement. In systems choked by politics, bureaucracy, collective-bargaining agreements, and institutionalized timidity, there is little incentive or opportunity to react to competition in these ways.

To get schools to respond more meaningfully to competitive pressure, incentives and rules must be changed in order to ensure that the competitive pressure is actually felt. Consider that today's charter schools get about 75 cents for every dollar that district schools receive, and that the per-pupil funding levels of the voucher programs in Washington, D.C., and Milwaukee amount to less than 50% of district per-pupil spending. This funding disparity prevents public-school alternatives from mounting serious challenges to traditional district schools.

Moreover, the D.C. voucher program capped enrollment at about 3% of the District of Columbia's student population, and there was no risk of monetary loss to the school district if students departed for private schools. Indeed, the compromise that allowed the voucher-program legislation to pass required that D.C. public schools receive additional funding, even as they would no longer bear the expense of educating the voucher students. The initial sum was an extra $13 million a year; this figure was eventually boosted to $40 million per year after Democrats took control of Congress in 2007.

Milwaukee's public schools have been similarly insulated from the consequences of losing students to the Milwaukee Parental Choice Program: Even as the tiny pilot grew from 337 participants in 1990 into a program that enrolls 20,000 students today, the Milwaukee public school system has remained largely unscathed. Since 1990, while enrollment has dipped, the district has boosted per-pupil spending by more than 80% (from $6,200 to more than $11,700), and increased the teacher workforce (from 5,554 to 5,768). This is choice without consequences—competition as soft political slogan rather than hard economic reality.

Making a Real Difference

As a result, despite hopes that school choice could "all by itself" bring about the other changes reformers have battled for, choice has not necessarily changed incentives or dynamics. Imagine a private-sector manager who knows that gaining or losing customers will have little or no impact on his salary, performance evaluations, or job security. Bizarre as it seems, this is exactly how "competition" generally works in K–12 education today. When a principal loses dozens of students, her evaluations, job prospects, and salary remain unaffected. And a principal who competes successfully is typically rewarded with nothing more than the joys of a more crowded cafeteria.

Of course, none of this is an indictment of school choice or of market-oriented reforms; rather, it suggests that much of our policy making to date has tended to reflect impassioned hopes instead of cool calculations. If every dollar spent on a student followed him when he changed schools—a state of affairs that exists nowhere in this country today—the verdict on choice-inspired competition would likely be quite different.

That difference would be sharper still if the laws and contracts that protect teacher and administrator jobs and salaries, and that handcuff managers, were changed—or if changes in school enrollment became a significant criterion for evaluating superintendents and principals.

The fiscal crunch in which many state and local governments now find themselves, or the moves in some jurisdictions to reform teacher tenure and pay, may make it possible to remove some of the insulation that has protected educators for so long. And because school districts are political entities, an exodus of students has the potential to spur useful change by altering the local political calculus. The departure of one-third of students to charter schools over the previous decade, for instance, helped create the conditions that led Washington, D.C., mayor Adrian Fenty to appoint the hard-charging Michelle Rhee as schools chancellor in 2007. For now, however, competition does not appear to much perturb most public school administrators—especially as many superintendents and school boards seem perfectly content to run slightly smaller districts with proportionally fewer dollars.

Choice Is Not Competition

The biggest mistake pro-market school reformers have made can thus be put simply: They have mistaken choice for competition. The conviction that school choice constitutes, by itself, a market solution has too often led reformers to skip past the hard work necessary to take advantage of the opportunities that choice-based reform can provide. Choice is merely part of the market equation; equally crucial are the requirements that market conditions permit high-quality or cost-effective suppliers to flourish, that regulation not smother new entrants, and that rules not require inefficient practices or subsidize also-rans.

Note that reformers rarely focus on "choice" when promoting market-based improvements to other sectors; in earlier decades, reformers didn't speak of "telecommunications choice" or "airline choice." Rather, they talked of "deregulation." Implicit was the understanding that deregulation involves more than the mere proliferation of options, that dynamic markets require much more than customers' choosing among government-operated programs and a handful of nonprofits, and that vacuums in a particular sector will not naturally or necessarily be filled by competent or virtuous actors. Whether dealing with nascent markets in Eastern Europe in the 1990s or the vagaries of energy deregulation, reformers have struggled to nurture the institutions, incentives, and practices that characterize healthy markets. Markets are a product of laws, norms, talent, information, and capital, and the absence of these can readily yield market failures—not because markets do not work, but because markets are not a magical salve.

Just as school improvement does not miraculously happen without attention to instruction, curriculum, and school leadership, so a rule-laden, risk-averse sector dominated by entrenched bureaucracies, industrial-style collective-bargaining agreements, and hoary colleges of education will not casually remake itself just because students have the right to switch schools. Happily, in recent years, a growing number of thoughtful scholars—like Andrew Coulson, John Merrifield, Terry Moe, Jay Greene, Patrick Wolf, and Paul Hill—have paid increasing attention to these questions of market structure and design. But such thinking remains the exception, not the rule.

Making Choice Work

So, taking account of all of this, does school choice "work"? The question needs to be answered in three parts. First, for poor parents trapped in dangerous and underperforming urban school systems, it is pretty clear that school choice works. The evidence is reasonably persuasive that access to private schools and charter schools increases the likelihood that their children will fare well on reading and math tests or graduate from high school. And even if those results do not materialize, the parents are more likely to be satisfied with their children's schools and to regard them as safe.

Second, school choice *can* help make possible more coherent, focused schools. When families and teachers are assigned to schools based upon geography or bureaucratic formulas, it becomes difficult to forge the kind of agreement needed to establish strong discipline or clear expectations. The opportunities that choice creates for school leaders to recruit like-minded teachers and families—and then to set clear norms around conduct, learning, and pedagogy—can be a powerful tool. Still, their impact ultimately depends on effective use by savvy school leaders—as these opportunities in themselves surely will not automatically yield better schools.

Third, it is far from clear that school choice will necessarily offer broad, systemic benefits. Choice has not inspired hordes of charter school operators to develop outstanding alternatives; there is no evidence that charter schools, on average across the nation, are better than district schools. Moreover, there is (at best) only very modest evidence that choice programs, in and of themselves, prompt school districts to become more productive or cost effective. There is, however, fairly clear evidence that school districts do respond under sufficient duress and that high-quality charter schools will emerge under the right conditions.

The path forward requires that choice advocates overcome the legacy of their inflated expectations and promises. The insistence that school choice simply "works" helped put a saleable, amiable face on the tough medicine that champions of school reforms sought to deliver—but often at the cost of silencing discussion about how to make choice-based reform work well. In fact, to even question the claim that "choice works" has frequently been deemed a betrayal by choice advocates; this has left the field to a coterie of enthusiasts eager to talk about moral urgency, but disinclined to address incentives or market dynamics.

The Social Justice Case for School Choice

On one level, the benefits of such smiley-face advocacy are plain to see. One need only look at the raft of strong-willed, pro-charter-school Democrats—figures like New York City schools chancellor Joel Klein or Colorado state senator Michael Johnston—to see how the choice mantra has helped to broaden and deepen the support for transformative change. It is also true that there has not been a major pullback in any place where choice has gained a foothold. Outside of the Obama administration's move to end the D.C. voucher program—a change imposed on the school district from the outside—nowhere have charter schooling, school voucher programs, or tuition tax credits been implemented and then lost favor.

At the same time, however, there has been little attention paid to the innate limitations of the "social justice" case for choice, even as a *political* strategy. For one thing, this approach immediately signals to the three-fourths of American parents whose children are not enrolled in inner-city schools that this debate is not about them. And given that only about one household in five even contains school-age children, choice proponents are pushing an agenda sure to seem disconnected from or even threatening to the vast majority of Americans.

Like the architects of the Great Society nearly half a century ago, choice advocates have an unfortunate habit of dismissing or denigrating middle-class voters who do not share their moral zeal. They ignore the genuine, practical worry that choice-based measures may adversely affect the property values of suburbanites who paid a premium to purchase homes

---

Charter School Accountability

Successful charter schools are more than a collection of great teachers and an effective curriculum. They are also nonprofit corporations that must operate with maximum efficiency in order to produce strong results despite funding disparities and facilities challenges unique to charter schools. They are multimillion-dollar start-up enterprises whose stakeholders are parents, taxpayers, and public authorities. Because they are public schools, charters are publicly accountable not just for academic results, but also for sound stewardship of public dollars. And as schools of choice, charter schools must satisfy families and students to earn their re-enrollment each year.

"A Framework for Operational Quality," National Consensus Panel on Charter School Operational Quality, May 2009.

---

in good districts or school zones, and the concerns of these homeowners that their children may find themselves crowded out of popular schools.

Poor Track Record of Supporting Choice

Perhaps not coincidentally, in roughly two dozen referenda across the country over the past few decades, voucher advocates have yet to record a single win. In fact, the annual poll in the Hoover Institution's choice-friendly journal *Education Next* has shown that popular support for vouchers declined by a third, from 45% to 31%, between 2007 and 2010.

Proponents can (and do) rightfully place much of the blame for this track record on ferocious opposition from teachers' unions, but they have also blithely ignored basic political reality and prudence. They need to stop hectoring suburbanites, ease up on the moral indignation, and start promoting reform that will credibly improve the quality and cost effectiveness of American education for more than a small slice of households.

If advocates of market-oriented school reform accept this diagnosis, they can take a number of steps to improve their practical and political prospects.

Improving the Prospects for Choice

First, they should get serious about markets as a way to promote cost efficiency. Given the fiscal straits school systems now face—and given that the country has just been through a monumental health care debate that focused on the problems with third-party purchasing and the lack of incentives for consumers to think about costs—it is peculiar that the power of markets to engender price competition remains so unexplored in education. School spending entails no direct contribution from parents, and parents currently gain nothing from choosing a more cost-effective school; as a result, administrators in charter, district, and private schools have less reason to take tough steps to adopt cost-saving technologies or practices. And yet the choice agenda neglects mechanisms that could reward price-conscious parents by permitting them to save dollars for other educational expenditures (such as college or tutoring) if they chose lower-cost school options.

Second, reformers should broaden the educational-choice discussion beyond "school" choice. The narrow vocabulary of school choice made more sense 20 years ago, when online tutoring and virtual schooling were the stuff of science fiction, and when homeschooling was still a curiosity. But in 2010, this language is profoundly limiting. In the health care debate, even the most ardent single-payer enthusiasts believed that patients should be free to make a series of choices among physicians and providers of care. Yet in education, the most expansive vision of choice asks parents to decide among schools A, B, and C. This kind of choice may appeal to urban parents eager to escape awful schools; it does little, however, for suburban parents who generally like their schools but would like to take advantage of customized or higher-quality math or foreign-language instruction. A promising solution would be to permit families to redirect a portion of the dollars spent on their children through the educational equivalent of a health savings account. Such a mechanism would help families address children's unmet needs (such as extra tutoring in difficult subjects, or advanced instruction in areas of particular aptitude); it would also allow niche providers to emerge, would foster price competition for particular services, and would make educational choice relevant to many more families.

The Role of For-Profit Education

Third, champions of market-based reform should stop downplaying the role of for-profit educators. The Obama administration has been particularly guilty on this count, enthusiastically championing charter school expansion even as its Department of Education radiates hostility toward for-profits in K–12 and higher education. The result is entrenched funding arrangements, policies, and political currents that stifle for-profit operators—organizations such as National Heritage Academies, which operates 67 charter schools in eight states, or EdisonLearning, which operates schools and provides supplemental education services across the United States and overseas. If choice-based reform is to yield more than boutique solutions, for-profits are a critical piece of the puzzle.

Consider that it has taken the celebrated KIPP [Knowledge Is Power Program] program—an organization lauded for its aggressive expansion—16 years to grow to 99 schools serving fewer than 27,000 students. This is longer than it took Microsoft, Subway, and Amazon to grow from start-ups to global brands. For-profits find it easier to tap private equity; they have self-interested reasons to aggressively seek cost efficiencies and to grow rapidly; and their focus on the bottom line can make them more willing to re-allocate resources when circumstances warrant a change. Of course, these same incentives can translate into corner-cutting and compromising quality; still, no one should imagine that nonprofits can readily match the dexterity, capacity for rapid growth and massive scale, and aggressive cost-cutting that are hallmarks of the for-profit sector.

Fourth, reformers should foster genuine competition by arranging markets so that there are real consequences for competitive failure or success. One simple step would be to ensure that all of the dollars spent on students follow children when they change schools (the notion implicit in efforts to promote "weighted student funding" systems). Such a reform would entail stripping school districts of their hefty subsidies and of their monopolies over local school facilities. It would mean overhauling contracts and statutes that protect teacher jobs and seniority-driven pay scales—practices that leave school and district leaders without the tools needed to reward good teachers and penalize mediocrity. Real consequences for enrollment loss could help push educational leaders to start taking enrollment and parental preferences seriously when evaluating employees and doling out bonuses. And, because school districts are politically governed entities, it would enable reformers to leverage student flight—as they have in Washington, D.C.—to create the pressure and political cover that public officials need to pursue painful, but essential, reforms.

Better Information Leads to Smarter Choices

Fifth, markets are predicated on the assumption that consumers have the ability to make informed choices. It is not essential for every single consumer to have the knowledge or inclination to make savvy decisions—but providers do need to expect that the quality of their performance will be known, and will matter. Today, unfortunately, it is enormously difficult for parents in most communities to get useful information on school quality. Simple test scores generally tell parents at least as much about the students attending the school in question as they do about the quality of instruction. Reliable measures of how much students learn during a year (i.e., the school's "value added") are infinitely more useful, but they are as yet available in only a handful of places for a limited number of schools, grades, and subjects. Similarly, it is difficult for parents to find comparable or trustworthy data on school safety, arts instruction, programs for high achievers, or the fate of former students. There is a gaping need for third parties to step up and play the role of a Zagat's guide or *Consumer Reports*, providing accessible, independent information on K–12 schools. As these examples make clear, there is absolutely value in having multiple providers, perhaps focusing on different educational concerns or kinds of schools. This area presents a vast opportunity for philanthropists or civic-minded enterprises, especially as promising but primitive information-distribution efforts already exist in cities like New Orleans, Milwaukee, and New Haven, Connecticut.

Finally, reformers should recognize that dynamic markets require vibrant entrepreneurial ecosystems. What has made Silicon Valley a locus of entrepreneurship is not that it has a "freer" marketplace than other American cities, but that it has attracted over decades the investors, researchers, and networked expertise necessary to develop and sustain high-quality ventures. Experience has made clear that such ecosystems don't necessarily spring into being unbidden, and that they sometimes need to be consciously cultivated. Even in choice hotbeds like Milwaukee and Washington [D.C.], we still do not see many growth-oriented providers or savvy investors screening potential new entrants and nurturing those with the most promise. Meanwhile, too little is being done to help new education providers find facilities, negotiate political obstacles, or leverage labor-saving technologies. Ventures like New Schools for New Orleans and the Mind Trust in Indianapolis represent pioneering efforts to clear bureaucratic obstacles, attract talent, and cultivate networks. Such efforts are multiplying across the land, spurred by supporters like the [Bill & Melinda] Gates Foundation and the NewSchools Venture Fund, and aided by federal policies like the Race to the Top program. These are promising developments—and they deserve more attention and care from reformers.

Periodical and Internet Sources Bibliography

The following articles have been selected to supplement the diverse views presented in this chapter.

Nick Anderson
"Study: Charter School Growth Accompanied by Racial Imbalance," *Washington Post*, February 4, 2010.

Howard Blume
"Charter Schools' Growth Promoting Segregation, Studies Say," *Los Angeles Times*, February 4, 2010.

Bob Braun
"Bringing N.J. Schools' Racial Segregation into Open," *Star-Ledger* (New Jersey), May 19, 2011.

Lindsey Burke
"National School Choice Week: It's Personal," *Deseret News* (Utah), January 22, 2011.

Conn Carroll
"The Union War on Charter Schools Annotated," *The Foundry* (blog), April 17, 2009. http://blog.heritage.org.

Paul Grogan
"Charter Schools' Time Has Come," *Patriot Ledger* (Massachusetts), October 26, 2009.

Bob Herbert
"Separate and Unequal," *New York Times*, March 21, 2011.

Jill Tucker
"Study: Segregation Rife at Charter Schools," *San Francisco Chronicle*, February 5, 2010.

Danny Weil
"Charter Schools: The White Man's Panacea for Education," *The Daily Censored* (blog), April 1, 2010. http://dailycensored.com.

Grover "Russ" Whitehurst
"Innovation, Motherhood, and Apple Pie," Brookings Institution, March 2009. www.brookings.edu.

Marcus A. Winters
"Charters' Promise," *City Journal*, September 28, 2009.

For Further Discussion

Chapter 1

1. There has been a serious debate in recent years about the success of charter schools in the United States. Read the viewpoints written by Ben Adams, Sarah Butrymowicz, and Diane Ravitch, three commentators who have different perspectives on the issue. Which viewpoint is the most persuasive and why?

2. Vicki E. Murray argues in her viewpoint that charter schools offer much-needed competition for traditional public schools. In what ways do you think charter schools can force regular schools to improve? Or do you disagree with Murray's thesis? Why?

Chapter 2

1. Are religious schools constitutional? Read viewpoints by Benjamin Siracusa Hillman and Susan Jacoby to inform your answer.

2. It has been charged that religious charters do not serve the common good and cater to a limited group of students. Grace Rauh points out that religious charters can provide a secular education and can appeal to a wide swath of parents. Charles C. Haynes argues that religious charters are inherently restrictive and put off many parents. After reading both viewpoints, what is your perspective on the issue?

3. Chester E. Finn Jr. and Michael Petrilli contend that failing urban Catholic schools should be converted into charter schools. Matthew Ladner maintains that Catholic schools should be saved through tax credits and other

measures. Do you think it is important to save urban Catholic schools? Why or why not?

Chapter 3

1. After reading the first five viewpoints in the chapter, what is your impression of online charter schools? Do you think that they are a viable alternative to traditional public schools? To brick-and-mortar charter schools? Why or why not?

2. Should online charter schools have the same funding as traditional public schools and charter schools? Read viewpoints by Weintana Abraha, Carol Pogash, and the Commonwealth Foundation to inform your answer.

3. In his viewpoint, David N. Bass discusses the growing concern homeschoolers have with online charter schools. Do you think such concerns are justified? Provide support for your position.

Chapter 4

1. Thomas Toch argues that there should be fewer charter schools. Marcus A. Winters suggests that a need for more charter schools exists. Read both viewpoints. Which viewpoint is more persuasive and why?

2. Racial segregation in charter schools has been a controversial issue in recent years. Read viewpoints by Noah Lederman, RiShawn Biddle, and Gary Ritter, Nathan Jensen, Brian Kisida, and Joshua McGee to find out more about the issue. Do you agree with Lederman that it is a pressing problem that needs to be addressed, or do you find that the issue has been overblown? Use information from the viewpoints to support your position.

Organizations to Contact

The editors have compiled the following list of organizations concerned with the issues debated in this book. The descriptions are derived from materials provided by the organizations. All have publications or information available for interested readers. The list was compiled on the date of publication of the present volume; names, addresses, phone and fax numbers, and e-mail and Internet addresses may change. Be aware that many organizations take several weeks or longer to respond to inquiries, so allow as much time as possible.

Achieve

1400 Sixteenth Street NW, Suite 510
Washington, DC   20036-2256
(202) 419-1540 • fax: (202) 828-0911
website: www.achieve.org

Achieve is an independent, nonpartisan organization concerned with passing effective and meaningful educational reform such as raising academic standards and strengthening accountability. In 2005 it launched the American Diploma Project Network, which brings together business executives, school officials, and politicians to align high school standards and assessment and accountability systems. The organization's annual report, *Closing the Expectations Gap*, monitors states' progress in reaching these goals. Achieve also conducts extensive research and publishes state and national reports in addition to policy briefs. It also publishes a monthly e-newsletter, *Perspective*, which focuses on current issues and provides updates on recent initiatives.

Center for Education Reform (CER)

910 Seventeenth Street NW, Suite 1120
Washington, DC   20006
(800) 521-2118 • fax: (301) 986-1826

e-mail: cer@edreform.com
website: www.edreform.com

The Center for Education Reform (CER) is a national organization dedicated to implementing effective educational reform. One of CER's main issues of interest is charter schools; the organization advocates for more high-quality charter schools in the United States and measures the success and accomplishments of public charter schools across the country. The CER website posts the latest research and press releases from the organization's experts; provides a forum for teachers, charter school authorizers, policy makers, and parents to discuss education issues; and offers a way for interested citizens to become involved in grassroots educational reform advocacy in their area. It also links to CER's annual survey of charter schools that evaluates the state of charter school education in the United States.

Center for Research on Education Outcomes (CREDO)
434 Galvez Mall, Stanford University
Stanford, CA   94305-6010
(650) 725-3431 • fax: (650) 723-1687
e-mail: credoatstanford@gmail.com
website: http://credo.stanford.edu

The Center for Research on Education Outcomes (CREDO) is a research center and think tank associated with Stanford University that focuses on compiling data on educational reform and student performance. CREDO works to provide innovative and effective educational reform policies and programs to improve the quality of American education. A key mission of CREDO is to publish national charter evaluations, which measure the success of charter schools in order to pinpoint policies and practices beneficial to the charter school movement. Some of CREDO's publications include *Not Condemned to Fail: An Analysis of California's Low Performing Schools*, *Paying for A's: An Early Exploration of Student Rewards and Incentive Programs in Charter Schools*, and *Multiple Choice: Charter School Performance in 16 States*.

International Association for K–12 Online Learning (iNACOL)

1934 Old Gallows Road, Suite 350, Vienna, VA   22182-4040
(888) 956-2265 • fax: (703) 752-6201
website: www.inacol.org

The International Association for K–12 Online Learning (iNACOL) is a nonprofit organization that advocates for increased access to quality online education programs. It facilitates the evaluation and dissemination of online learning programs, develops standards, and lobbies for policies that increase access and improve quality. The organization also assists in funding efforts for various online programs and provides a forum for administrators and participants to exchange ideas about how to improve and maintain the quality of virtual education. Some of these events include lectures, presentations, webinars, and symposiums. The iNACOL website links to a number of relevant reports and research publications and hosts a forum that posts the latest news in the industry.

National Alliance for Public Charter Schools

1101 Fifteenth Street NW, Suite 1010, Washington, DC   20005
(202) 289-2700 • fax: (202) 289-4009
website: www.publiccharters.org

The National Alliance for Public Charter Schools is a nonprofit organization that works to support the spread of charter schools across the country, particularly in areas that could benefit from school choice. The organization advocates for charter school students, parents, teachers, and administrators with policy makers and politicians with the goal of passing legislation beneficial to the charter school movement and creating policies that will increase access to charter schools. One of the organization's aims is to eliminate "charter caps" that limit the number of charter schools in certain areas. The National Alliance of Public Charter Schools often works with state charter school associations and resource centers to develop high-quality charter schools. The group's website provides fact sheets, reports and research, and a multimedia library that includes photos, videos, and audio recordings of recent events, speeches, and presentations.

National Association of Charter School Authorizers (NACSA)

105 W. Adams Street, Suite 3500, Chicago, IL   60603-6253
(312) 376-2300 • fax: (312) 376-2400
e-mail: loreleic@qualitycharters.org
website: www.qualitycharters.org

The National Association of Charter School Authorizers (NACSA) is an organization that "is devoted exclusively to improving public education by improving the policies and practices of the organizations responsible for authorizing charter schools." NACSA develops and applies standards of excellence for charter schools, provides resources and guidance for charter school authorizers, and funds promising and innovative programs and policies. NACSA also organizes an annual leadership conference that offers a valuable opportunity for charter school authorizers to network, exchange ideas, attend leadership and training sessions, and listen to leaders in the charter school movement. A number of NACSA publications are available online through the organization's website, including reports, issue briefs, and policy guides.

National Charter Schools Institute (NCSI)

2520 University Park Drive, Mount Pleasant, MI   48858
(989) 774-2999 • fax: (989) 774-2591
e-mail: info@nationalcharterschools.org
website: www.nationalcharterschools.org

The National Charter Schools Institute (NCSI) is a nonprofit organization that works with charter school authorizers, boards, school leaders, policy makers, educators, and others to improve charter school curricula and student performance. NCSI identifies and implements effective programs and policies and works to support successful charter schools across the nation. It also provides management training for charter school leaders, offers a forum for networking and exchanging ideas, and disseminates the latest news and research on the charter school movement. The NCSI website provides updates on recent initiatives and events; a news and video archive; breaking news alerts; and essential information for parents, educators, boards, authorizers, and charter school management. There is also an online store to purchase NCSI's latest publications.

National Education Association (NEA)

1201 Sixteenth Street NW, Washington, DC   20036
(202) 833-4000 • fax: (202) 822-7974
website: www.nea.org

Founded in 1857, the National Education Association (NEA) is the largest labor union in the United States. The NEA represents more than 3.2 million public school teachers, school employees, college instructors and staffers, and retired educators. The association's mission is "to advocate for education professionals and to unite our members and the nation to fulfill the promise of public education to prepare every student to succeed in a diverse and interdependent world." The NEA's activities range from raising money for scholarship programs to developing training and leadership programs for teachers and lobbying for appropriate levels of school funding from local, state, and federal governments. NEA Today is a website that offers the latest stories on education topics, as well as access to the *NEA Today* magazine. The NEA also publishes *Thought & Action*, a journal focused on education theory; *Tomorrow's Teachers*, a resource for teachers; and *Higher Education Advocate*, a bimonthly newsletter that explores issues important in higher education.

Public Education Network (PEN)

601 Thirteenth Street NW, Suite 710 South
Washington, DC   20005-3808
(202) 628-7460
e-mail: pen@publiceducation.org
website: www.publiceducation.org

The Public Education Network (PEN) is an independent, national association of local education funds and individuals working together to advance effective public school reform with the mission of improving public education in low-income communities. One of the organization's key tasks is to disseminate information about innovative school reform and quality educational programs around the country. To accomplish this, PEN publishes policy briefs, fact sheets, research papers, in-depth studies, and reports on subjects such as No Child Left Behind (NCLB), teacher resources, and new funding initiatives and strategies. It also publishes a weekly e-newsletter found on its website, which features op-eds, press releases, and research on relevant school funding issues.

US Department of Education

400 Maryland Avenue SW, Washington, DC   20202
(800) 872-5327
website: www.ed.gov

The US Department of Education is the federal department that establishes federal school funding policies, distributes funds, monitors school performance, and enforces federal law on discrimination. It also distributes financial aid to eligible students and oversees research on America's school in order to determine the success of educational programs across the country. After careful expert analysis of data, the department then makes well-considered recommendations for school reform. There are a range of publications available on the department's website, including handbooks, research papers, speeches, congressional testimony, and in-depth studies on reform and funding topics. It also publishes a number of journals and newsletters, including *Education Research News, ED-Info*, and *Education Innovator*.

Bibliography of Books

Thomas M. Bloch — *Stand for the Best: What I Learned After Leaving My Job as CEO of H&R Block to Become a Teacher and Founder of an Inner-City Charter School.* San Francisco, CA: Jossey-Bass, 2008.

Jack Buckley and Mark Schneider — *Charter Schools: Hope or Hype?* Princeton, NJ: Princeton University Press, 2007.

Patricia Burch — *Hidden Markets: The New Education Privatization.* New York: Routledge, 2009.

Lucas A. Camilleri, ed. — *District of Columbia Schools: Reform Progress.* Hauppauge, NY: Nova Science Publishers, 2011.

Ronald G. Corwin and E. Joseph Schneider — *The School Choice Hoax: Fixing America's Schools.* Lanham, MD: Rowman & Littlefield, 2007.

Maurice R. Dyson and Daniel B. Weddle, eds. — *Our Promise: Achieving Educational Equality for America's Children.* Durham, NC: Carolina Academic Press, 2009.

Kent A. Farnsworth — *Grassroots School Reform: A Community Guide to Developing Globally Competitive Students.* New York: Palgrave Macmillan, 2010.

Erica Frankenberg and Elizabeth Debray, eds. — *Integrating Schools in a Changing Society: New Policies and Legal Options for a Multiracial Generation.* Chapel Hill: University of North Carolina Press, 2011.

Paul T. Hill — *Learning as We Go: Why School Choice Is Worth the Wait.* Stanford, CA: Education Next, 2010.

Richard D. Kahlenberg — *Tough Liberal: Albert Shanker and the Battles over Schools, Unions, Race, and Democracy.* New York: Columbia University Press, 2007.

Anthony Kelly — *School Choice and Student Well-Being: Opportunity and Capability in Education.* New York: Palgrave Macmillan, 2007.

Carol Klein — *Virtual Charter Schools and Home Schooling.* Youngstown, NY: Cambria Press, 2006.

Myron Lieberman — *The Educational Morass: Overcoming the Stalemate in American Education.* Lanham, MD: Rowman & Littlefield, 2007.

Christopher A. Lubienski and Peter C. Weitzel, eds. — *The Charter School Experiment: Expectations, Evidence, and Implications.* Cambridge, MA: Harvard Education Press, 2010.

Michael Manley-Casimir and Kirsten Manley-Casimir, eds. — *The Courts, the Charter, and the Schools: The Impact of the Charter of Rights and Freedoms on Educational Policy and Practice, 1982–2007.* Toronto: University of Toronto Press, 2009.

Katherine K. Merseth et al. — *Inside Urban Charter Schools: Promising Practices and Strategies in Five High-Performing Schools.* Cambridge, MA: Harvard Education Press, 2009.

Janet D. Mulvey, Bruce S. Cooper, and Arthur T. Maloney — *Blurring the Lines: Charter, Public, Private and Religious Schools Coming Together.* Charlotte, NC: Information Age Publishing, 2010.

Karin Piper — *Charter Schools: The Ultimate Handbook for Parents.* Deadwood, OR: Wyatt-MacKenzie, 2009.

Jeanne M. Powers — *Charter Schools: From Reform Imagery to Reform Reality.* New York: Palgrave Macmillan, 2009.

Oliver M. Prisser, ed. — *Charter Schools: Impact and Grant Challenges.* Hauppauge, NY: Nova Science Publishers, 2011.

Diane Ravitch — *The Death and Life of the Great American School System: How Testing and Choice Are Undermining Education.* New York: Basic Books, 2010.

Danny Weil   *Charter School Movement: History,*
                          Politics, Policies, Economics and
                          Effectiveness. 2nd ed. Amenia, NY:
                          Grey House Publishing, 2009.

Lawrence D.   *Religious Charter Schools: Legalities*
Weinberg   *and Practicalities.* Charlotte, NC:
                          Information Age Publications, 2007.

Richard Whitmire   *The Bee Eater: Michelle Rhee Takes on*
                          the Nation's Worst School District. San
                          Francisco, CA: Jossey-Bass, 2011.

Deb Yoder and   *Charter Schools: Moving to the Next*
Judy Rooney   *Level.* Bloomington, IN:
                          AuthorHouse, 2007.

Index